———— Dr. Elin Riegel

THE

SUCCESS

CONTRACT

Without Fine Print

A Whole New Perspective on the Blood Covenant

The Success Contract—Without Fine Print
A Whole New Perspective on the Blood Covenant

© Copyright 2015 – Elin Riegel

ISBN (Print): 978-84-606-5847-4

ISBN (Kindle): 978-84-606-5848-1

Published in Spain.

Cover Design, Typesetting and Preparation for Publication by
Palm Tree Publishing: www.palmtreeproductions.com

For Worldwide Distribution

1 2 3 4 5 6 / 18 17 16 15

To contact the author:

www.wiministries.com

Dedication

I dedicate this book to all my students throughout the past 18 years who really made me dig into this tremendous revelation, resulting in the teaching you have in your hands today.

I also dedicate this book to you, who may be just now becoming a student of the powerful Word of God, to help you get hold of the kind of security, authority, and success that God has built into you from the beginning, to apply it, and to be able to live by it.

Acknowledgments

I acknowledge my very supportive and collaborating family. My daughter Aina Riegel who has been hands-on helping with the practical side of this book, my son-in-law Christopher Andersson for going through the manuscript and correcting my English, and also to my daughter Nina for her encouragement and support.

To my employees in World Impact Ministries Spain who have been after me for years to write a book on this topic.

Also thanks to Dr. Keith Johnson for getting me started and putting me in contact with his excellent editor.

Thank you to my editor, Angela Rickabaugh Shears for getting me through the editing process in an efficient and professional way.

Praise for The Success Contract

"Wow! What a great book on the importance of understanding COVENANT. I have a success contract with God! This is a powerful statement and the book is a must read for those who are serious about making a significant impact in the world. Your success is guaranteed. You don't have to live a life of hopelessness anymore.

Everything God has belongs to you through COVENANT. This book will give you the confidence to keep moving forward so you can achieve your God-given destiny ... God's ultimate desire for your life."

Dr. Keith Johnson

America's #1 Confidence Coach

www.keithjohnson.tv

Writing about the blood covenant cannot be attempted without serious study of the subject, and a working knowledge of the power and authority therein. Elin Riegel has provided both in her anointed new book, *The Success Contract*.

God's will for our lives is nothing short of total victory and complete success in our endeavors to accomplish His purposes in this world. With the knowledge of the blood covenant and the practical applications revealed in this book, both are guaranteed. The blood covenant we have with God through Christ assures us that we are backed with every resource God has to overcome evil forces and advance the Kingdom of God on Earth.

Without this revelation knowledge, God's people will live on the low plane of "behavior modification" and not in "world overcoming faith"—the realm where demonstrations of the Spirit and power are common occurrences in our lives. As you read this book, you will learn why Christ was legally authorized to take our place in judgement, and how we now can take His place as ambassadors of reconciliation and deliverance to all peoples.

Thanks to Elin for the many years of the study and practice of blood covenant truths. All who read this book will find liberty in daily life, and a great resource for making disciples of Jesus Christ.

Dr. John Polis

International Ambassador, International Coalition of Apostolic Leaders

Founder/President, Revival Fellowship International

www.rfiusa.org

Contents

Introduction

After more than twenty years living with the Blood Covenant in my personal life, service and ministry, and teaching it in my Bible schools and Leader Academy, the Lord said it was time to share this revelation in the form of a book.

It is my strong desire to share this tremendous revelation with you, my brother or sister in the Kingdom, as it is so life-changing, revolutionary, and still as current today as in Biblical times. The commission from God to write this book came with a clear order to make this "Success Contract" with God applicable in our daily lives.

The Hebrew Blood Covenant, or contract if you like, is hidden throughout the Scriptures from Genesis to Revelation; because it was such a common knowledge among all people in biblical times, very little is explained in detail by the authors of the Bible.

The only place we really see some details is in Genesis 15:17, where God cut a Blood Covenant with Abraham, a success contract written in blood: "And it came to pass, when the sun went down and it was dark, that behold, there appeared a smoking oven and a burning torch that passed between those pieces." I contend that much more explanation is desperately needed for you and me and the church in general, to get hold of the tremendous implications the Blood Covenant has for us today.

Let me challenge you: if you do not understand the impact and the principles of the Old Testament and the New Testament Blood Covenants, you will not really understand the Bible, the living Word of God. And how can you apply and use these principles if you do not understand them? If you do not have this revelation crystal clear in your heart and mind, you will never ever be able to enter into and live out the abundant and successful life that our Lord Jesus prepared for you.

Are you ready to have your life changed? Allow me to start with the very beginning; we need to build this terrific house on a solid foundation so it will work forever in your life from now on.

Chapter One

Why Blood?

L et me start with a couple of questions:

- What gave Jesus Christ the right to take our sins and curses on His own body?

- The Bible has thousands of promises for us, how do we know that they are true and trustworthy?

Have you ever asked yourself these questions? Well I did, from the beginning of my walk in the Kingdom. I am a very practical person, and I could not just accept the phrases in First Peter 2:24 that say that He bore our sins, and in Galatians 3:13 where it says that He took our curses. *Why?* What gave Him the right to do that, and how do I know that it is true?

I know that God is Almighty, but He is also righteous; He follows the rules that He sets.

An example of this is that He has given us as human beings a free will. He will never overrule that and make you do something you don't want to do. In the same way, He will follow His own rules when it comes to everything else. God's rule about sin is that the wages of sin is death (see Romans 6:23), so *I* should have been hanging on that cross.

If Jesus could take my sins and curses, there had to be something that gave Him the *right* to do so. Some way God could let Jesus take my sins and curses without breaking His own rules.

And if my sins and curses were really taken away by Him, I wanted to know where, how, and which chapter and verse in the Word of God I could find that truth! Did you know that God does not have a problem with us asking for these kinds of confirmations? He delights in His children digging deeper into His Word.

As you will see, God gave me all the answers I needed through the revelation that I am about to share with you.

What Is the Blood Covenant?

- A blood covenant is an unbreakable contract for personal success.

- A blood covenant, *berit* in Hebrew, is an extremely strong agreement between two or more parties, where blood is shed as a token of the covenant. Blood is always a symbol of life itself.

- A blood covenant always invokes blessings and curses. There were and are blessings for honoring it and curses for breaking it.

- A blood covenant is the strongest agreement and relationship that was, is and will ever be.

- A blood covenant or contract meant: All that a person was and all that he had, belonged to his blood covenant partner until the death of one of the parties and even beyond death, caring for his family.

- A blood covenant was and is a very serious matter of life and death. It was respected and honored by all people.

We can find 250 references to blood covenants or contracts more or less hidden throughout the Bible. For example, Jacob offered a covenant sacrifice on the mountain and then called others to eat bread with him (see Genesis 31:54). The Passover blood covenant is referred to throughout the Bible and specifically in Exodus 12:27, *"It is the Passover sacrifice of the Lord, who passed over the houses of the children of Israel in Egypt when He struck the Egyptians and delivered our households.'"* In the New Testament, Matthew, Mark and Luke all record Jesus stating the power of His blood that would be shed for all who believe—see Matthew 26:28; Mark 14:24; Luke 22:20.

The Success Contract

The book of Hebrews reveals how eternally important the *"blood of the covenant"* is in knowing the truth of living daily within a contract of success with God:

*Therefore not even the first covenant
was dedicated without blood.*
Hebrews 9:18

*Saying, "This is the blood of the covenant
which God has command you."*
Hebrews 9:20

*Of how much worse punishment, do you suppose, will he be
thought worthy who has trampled the Son of God underfoot,
counted the blood of the covenant by which he was sanctified
a common thing, and insulted the Spirit of grace?*
Hebrews 10:29

*To Jesus the Mediator of the new covenant, and to the
blood of sprinkling better things than that of Abel.*
Hebrews 12:24

*Now may the God of peace who brought up our Lord
Jesus from the dead, that great Shepherd of the sheep,
through the blood of the everlasting covenant.*
Hebrews 13:20

Let us look at some more Bible references where can find blood covenants or contracts more or less hidden. Some of them you might not understand as covenants, but as we start going through the Hebrew blood covenant rituals, you will see them very clearly. Remember that when the Bible was written, *everyone* knew what it was, and the smallest hint would tell the reader that here a covenant had been or was being cut.

> *And the Lord restored Job's losses when he prayed for his friends. Indeed the Lord gave Job twice as much as he had before. Then all his brothers, all his sisters, and all those who had been his acquaintances before, came to him and ate food with him in his house; and they consoled him and comforted him for all the adversity that the Lord had brought upon him. Each one gave him a piece of silver and each a ring of gold.*
>
> ### Job 42:10-11

> *Then Jonathan and David made a covenant, because he loved him as his own soul. And Jonathan took off the robe that was on him and gave it to David, with his armor, even to his sword and his bow and his belt.*
>
> ### 1 Samuel 18:3-4

> *So he departed from there, and found Elisha the son of Shaphat, who was plowing with twelve yoke of oxen before him, and he was with the twelfth. Then Elijah passed by him and threw his mantle on him.*
>
> ### 1 Kings 19:19

Then Melchizedek king of Salem brought out bread and wine; he was the priest of God Most High.
Genesis 14:18

Then he brought all these to Him and cut them in two, down the middle, and placed each piece opposite the other; but he did not cut the birds in two.
Genesis 15:10

Thus they made a covenant at Beersheba. So Abimelech rose with Phichol, the commander of his army, and they returned to the land of the Philistines. Then Abraham planted a tamarisk tree in Beersheba, and there called on the name of the Lord, the Everlasting God. And Abraham stayed in the land of the Philistines many days.
Genesis 21:32-34

No longer do I call you servants, for a servant does not know what his master is doing; but I have called you friends, for all things that I heard from My Father I have made known to you.
John 15:15

I do not pray for these alone, but also for those who will believe in Me through their word; that they all may be one, as You, Father, are in Me, and I in You;

that they also may be one in Us, that the world may believe that You sent Me. And the glory which You gave Me I have given them, that they may be one just as We are one: I in them, and You in Me; that they may be made perfect in one, and that the world may know that You have sent Me, and have loved them as You have loved Me. "Father, I desire that they also whom You gave Me may be with Me where I am, that they may behold My glory which You have given Me; for You loved Me before the foundation of the world. O righteous Father! The world has not known You, but I have known You; and these have known that You sent Me. And I have declared to them Your name, and will declare it, that the love with which You loved Me may be in them, and I in them"

John 17:20-26

You will find these kinds of references in about 240 more places. They are there! You just didn't know about them because you didn't know the blood covenant. But that is about to change.

We will be studying a typical Hebrew blood covenant from the times of the Bible and today's applications and functions of it. You will soon understand the extended application of success for you today!

Who Initiated the Blood Covenant?

To understand who initiated the blood covenant, we have to start at the beginning. We find the first blood covenant way back in the Word of God, in Genesis 3:21, *"Also for Adam and his wife the Lord God made **tunics of skin**, and clothed them."* Even though Adam and Eve sinned against God—disobeyed by eating from the tree of the knowledge of good and evil—He provided clothing for them.

Where did those *"tunics of skin"* come from? We see that God Himself killed, sacrificed an animal, shedding lifeblood, to make a covenant with humanity. Adam and Eve had sinned, and God forgave them and covered them, giving them protection for a certain time. The humans had "died" spiritually, so God "covered" them spiritually with the blood of another living creature.

Biblically speaking, blood always carries life—without blood there is no life.

*For **the life of the flesh is in the blood**, and I have given it to you upon the altar to make atonement for your souls; for it is the blood that makes atonement for the soul.*
Leviticus 17:11

So who initiated the covenant? *God initiated the blood covenant, not humankind.*

Why Blood?

Do you know the story of Cain and Abel revealed in Genesis 4:9-10? God told Cain that the blood of Abel was crying out to Him from the ground. To God, the life of Abel was still in his blood after death.

If we take the blood covenant that the Lord made with humankind seriously, we will come to know life abundantly—spiritual, physical, relational, financial, mental, and emotional success will be ours.

- Spiritually we will mature to the point where we obey God without questions. Like Abraham when God asked him to sacrifice his son Isaac obeyed without understanding why. He only knew God would have to either save Isaac or raise him from the dead, because of the blood covenant. Sometimes God will ask us to do things without giving us an explanation, and we need to be willing to obey in the certainty that He loves unconditionally and wants the best for our lives.

> **Sometimes God will ask us to do things without giving us an explanation. Spiritually we will mature to the point where we obey God without questions.**

- Physically we will know that by His stripes we *are healed:* "*But He was wounded for our transgressions,*

11

He was bruised for our iniquities; the chastisement for our peace was upon Him, and by His stripes we **are healed***"* (Isaiah 53:5) and *"who Himself bore our sins in His own body on the tree, that we, having died to sins, might live for righteousness—by whose stripes you* **were healed***"* (First Peter 2:24). Notice that the Word of God doesn't say we might be healed or maybe we will be healed, no, it says we are healed and were healed—present and past tense—it is part of the blood covenant between us and Jesus Christ our Savior.

- We can know for certain that our relationships can be stronger and more abundantly fruitful than ever before if we rely on His promises: *"Let your conduct be without covetousness; be content with such things as you have. For He Himself has said, "I will never leave you nor forsake you"* (Hebrews 13:5).

- Financially and mentally we can rest assured that God will provide for us, always, and we can be at peace knowing that He is in control: *"Therefore I say to you,* **do not worry about your life,** *what you will eat or what you will drink; nor about your body, what you will put on. Is not life more than food and the body more than clothing? ...Which of you by worrying can add one cubit to his stature? ...Therefore do not worry...* **for your heavenly Father knows that you need all these things***"* (Matthew 6:25-32).

- Emotionally, we are given the power to control situations and emotions that are normally "too hot to handle." By knowing that the Holy Spirit dwells within us and allowing Him to guide our reactions, we can be shining examples for others, especially non-believers, of God's grace and mercy. *"But You are God, ready to pardon, gracious and merciful, slow to anger, abundant in kindness, and did not forsake them"* (Nehemiah 9:17). *"But you shall receive power when the Holy Spirit has come upon you; and you shall be witnesses to Me..."* (Acts 1:8).

The Hebrew Success Contract with God

The people in biblical times did not use written contracts or business agreements; rather, they made promises in front of witnesses. There had to be at least two witnesses, and they had to be Jewish, male, and over the age of 20. Women, the deaf, the crazy, blind, relatives, and slaves were not accepted as witnesses.

In the case of contracts being made, the witnesses would usually be the elders. The elders were the consulting body of the city or nation, and would hold their meetings near the city gate, in the square located next to the gate.[1] The gate was the business center of the city where all commercial and legal actions were conducted.

The Success Contract

Many times a sign would be used between two men such as a handshake or removing and handing over his shoe.

A man devoid of understanding shakes hands in
a pledge, and becomes surety for his friend.
Proverbs 17:18

Do not be one of those who shakes hands in a
pledge, one of those who is surety for debts.
Proverbs 22:26

Now this was the custom in former times in Israel
concerning redeeming and exchanging, to confirm
anything: one man took off his sandal and gave it to
the other, and this was a confirmation in Israel.
Ruth 4:7

A breach of an oral contract would mean a breach of faith. The person would lose his reputation and it would be said over him: "He who punished the generation of the Flood and of the Dispersion will exact payment from the one who does not stand by his Word."[2]

This is why the Bible talks about the importance of having a "good name." To us it is beneficial to have a good name, but in biblical times it was essential. The value of your name decided what business deals you obtained.

A good name is to be chosen rather than great
riches, loving favor rather than silver and gold.
Proverbs 22:1

Why Blood?

A good name is better than precious ointment, and
the day of death than the day of one's birth.
Ecclesiastes 7:1

The value of their name, their honesty and integrity was what counted.

For instance, when Moses led the Israelites out of Egypt, he assumed the role of leader, which included solving disputes among hundreds of thousands of people. His father-in-law, Jethro, saw the toll this heavy responsibility was having on Moses, he asked "Why do you alone sit, and all the people stand before you from morning until evening?" Moses replied:

"Because the people come to me to inquire of God. When they
have a difficulty, they come to me, and I judge between one and
another; and I make known the statutes of God and His laws."
Exodus 18:14-16

Then Jethro offered a brilliant suggestion to Moses:

"...you shall select from all the people able men, such
as fear God, men of truth, hating covetousness; and
place such over them to be rulers of thousands, rulers
of hundreds, rulers of fifties, and rulers of tens. And
let them judge the people at all times. Then it will be
that every great matter they shall bring to you, but
every small matter they themselves shall judge. ...If
you do this thing, and God so commands you, then

15

you will be able to endure, and all this people will
also go to their place in peace."
Exodus 18:21-23

Successful contracts of any type are sealed in "good faith" between two people, organizations, ministries, etc. Blood covenants, taken seriously, are deep commitments that affect those involved initially—and also affect generations to follow. Christians especially must be aware of the significance of entering into any covenant. It is vital that we know all there is to know about the other person, organization, ministry, etc. before bonding in any way. "Due diligence" is when we take time to research and analyze a person, business, or organization in preparation for a transaction.

> **Covenants are serious business. Christians must be aware of the significance of entering into any covenant.**

Harkening back to Jethro's advice, God commands us to choose carefully those with whom we transact, selecting only *"able men* [and women], *such as fear God, men* [and women] *of truth, hating covetousness."* Able people are those who have the ability to follow through when honoring their word and their commitments; God-fearing people know their priorities and set God above the minutia of life and focus on His will and plan; truth-tellers are those who will not compromise their integrity and are no way associated with the father of lies, Satan; people who hate covetousness are not greedy, materialistic, or envious. In today's instant-gratification world, it may take us some extra time and effort to find those who *"hate covetousness."*

Let's look back at the initial blood covenant and how it continues to work in millions of lives centuries after God's first act of mercy toward His children.

Benefits of the Blood Covenant

Why it is so important to understand today how a blood covenant works? The following are just a few reasons:

- To understand the Word of God. There are so many things in the Bible that seem strange without this revelation. Small phrases you never understood will now make sense.

- To understand your rights as a child of God. Many people live below par as Christians when God has given His *all* for us to have it all through our Covenant with Him.

- Understanding why marriage is so special.

- Understanding about why various intimate partners affects people's lives.

- And many more...

In addition to the most magnanimous gift of all—our eternal salvation, God's blood covenant with us has other benefits. Through Jesus' sacrifice we have freedom, healing and restoration. The heart of this ministry (World Impact Ministries) is not to cast out demons, but to close the doors so that they cannot enter. We focus on healing the brokenhearted and declaring liberty to those bound by misuse and abuse in all its ugly forms. Many people have had bad experiences with different ministries that minister deliverance, but God has shown us a very soft, quiet and beautiful way of ministering to people.

Throughout the book, we will discuss in more detail the benefits of the New Blood Covenant and how you can claim His promises and profits for yourself—and for those you love. When you sign on the dotted line of your personalized success contract, it leads you into a life filled with peace, joy, beauty, security, self-acceptance, love for others, good health, a forgiving nature, beauty, and freedom. But don't just take my word for it—take God's word for it—every truth is confirmed in the Bible.

So why the blood, as the chapter title asks? Because there is life in the blood, and you were born into this world at this particular time and in your particular place to live and love and share God's good news. You will be like a tree planted by living rivers of water, that brings forth nourishing fruit in the proper season, whose leaves will not wither; and whatever you do will prosper (see Psalm 1:3).

Why Blood?

From the Old Blood Covenant we read:

*For the life of the flesh is in the blood, and I have given it
to you upon the altar to make atonement for your souls;
for it is the blood that makes atonement for the soul.*

Leviticus 17:11

From the New Blood Covenant, Jesus says:

*"Whoever eats My flesh and drinks My blood has
eternal life, and I will raise him up at the last day."*

John 6:54

Hallelujah!

Endnotes

1. www.jewishvirtuallibrary.org.
2. ibid.

The Success Contract

Chapter Two

Types of Blood Covenants

In Hebrew times, counting 4,000 years of the Old Testament until the birth of Jesus, we find three different kinds of blood covenants:

1. Between God and a human or a group of humans

2. Between two people

3. Between a leader and a people

A blood covenant was normally cut between a stronger and a weaker party. The weaker needed the protection of the stronger, and the stronger normally wanted something that the weaker had, like money, property, or talents. Interestingly, sometimes we see in the Scripture that blood is being sacrificed, but not always.

1. As examples of covenants between God and a person, there are several rather well-known:

   • In Genesis 2:16-17 **between God and Adam:** *"And the Lord God commanded the man, saying, 'Of every tree of the garden you may freely eat; but of the tree of knowledge of good and evil you shall not eat, for in the day that you eat of it you shall surely die.'"*

   • In Genesis 9:1-17 **between God and Noah:** *"So God blessed Noah and his sons, and said to them: '... Surely for your lifeblood I will demand a reckoning.... And as for Me, behold, I establish My covenant with you and with your descendants after you.... I set My rainbow in the cloud, and it shall be for the sign of the covenant between Me and the earth....This is the sign of the covenant which I have established between Me and all flesh that is on the earth.'"*

   • In Genesis 15:8-21 **between God and Abraham:** *"...On the same day the Lord made a covenant with Abram, saying: 'To your descendants I have given this land ...'"* (Also see Genesis 12:1-3.)

   • In Genesis 28:13-22 **between God and Isaac:** *"And behold, the Lord stood above it and said: 'I am the Lord God of Abraham your father and the God of Isaac; the land on which you lie I will give to you and your descendants....'"*

- In Exodus 24:1-9 **between God and Moses**: *"Now He said to Moses, 'Come up to the Lord, you and Aaron…and worship from afar.' …And Moses took the blood, sprinkled it on the people, and said, 'This is the blood of the covenant which the Lord has made with you according to all these words.'"*

- In Psalm 89:3-4,28-29,34, and 37 **between God and David:** *"I have made a covenant with My chosen, I have sworn to My servant David…. My mercy I will keep for him forever, and My covenant shall stand firm with him…. My covenant I will not break, nor alter the word that has gone out of My lips. It shall be established forever like the moon, even like the faithful witness in the sky."*

2. As a blood covenant between two men, there are several examples:

- In 1 Samuel 18:3-5 **between David and Jonathan:** *"Then Jonathan and David made a covenant, because he loved him as his own soul. And Jonathan took off the robe that was on him and gave it to David, with his armor, even to his sword and his bow and his belt."*

- In 1 Kings 19:19-21 **between Elijah and Elisha:** *"So he departed from there, and found Elisha the son of Shaphat, who was plowing with twelve yoke of oxen before him, and he was with the twelfth. Then Elijah passed by him and threw his mantle on him. And he left the oxen and ran after Elijah, and said, "Please let me kiss my father and my mother, and then I will follow you."And he said to him,*

"Go back again, for what have I done to you?" So Elisha turned back from him, and took a yoke of oxen and slaughtered them and boiled their flesh, using the oxen's equipment, and gave it to the people, and they ate. Then he arose and followed Elijah, and became his servant"

There is mention of a blood covenant in Job 41 and 42, between Job and his friends, renewing their vows.

3. Covenants between a leader and his people also have many examples:

    • In Joshua 24:1-28 **between Joshua and the people of Israel:** *"Then Joshua gathered all the tribes of Israel to Shechem and called for the elders of Israel.... And the people said to Joshua, 'The Lord our God we will serve, and His voice we will obey!' So Joshua made a covenant with the people that day, and made for them a statute and an ordinance in Shechem...."*

    • In Ezra 10:30 **between Ezra and the people of Israel:** *"Now therefore, let us make a covenant with our God to put away all these wives and those who have been born to them, according to the advice of my master and of those who tremble at the commandment of our God; and let it be done according to the law."*

    • In 2 Kings 23:3 **between Josiah and the people of Israel:** *"Then the king stood by a pillar and made a covenant before the Lord, to follow the Lord and to keep His commandments and His testimonies and His* *statutes, with all his heart and all his soul, to perform the words of this covenant that were written in this book. And all the people took a stand for the covenant."*

- In 2 Chronicles 29:10 **between Hezekiah and the people of Israel:** *"Now it is in my heart to make a covenant with the Lord God of Israel, that His fierce wrath may turn away from us."*

After we study the blood covenant rituals, we will come back to a couple of these biblical examples. Without understanding the rituals, the examples will not make much sense.

These are some of the Old Testament blood covenants. The New Testament blood covenants and the work of the Lord Jesus are explained in Chapter 8.

Blood Covenants Today

Although not as prevalent today as in earlier times, there have been different types of blood covenants worldwide throughout the ages even until today. There are both genuine covenants and covenants that have been perverted into corruptible acts.

For example, every time a new tribe is discovered in the world, it is learned that they practice a form of a blood covenant. Primitive tribes in Africa, South America, and India that have been discovered, not having had any contact with civilization, had been practicing forms of blood covenant rituals, including drinking blood or cutting each other till blood flowed, etc.

Worldwide today there are also satanic blood sacrifices and rituals that involve dismemberment of animals and worse. These are perversions of the biblical blood covenant.

Missionaries should receive deserved recognition for bringing the New Testament Word of God to nations where human—men, women, and children—sacrifices were, and sometimes still are, commonplace. Many missionaries risked their lives to stop the brutal murders of innocents by shining the light of the Lord into dark and sinister beliefs based on fear and trying to satisfy the gods' bloodthirsty appetites. A Scottish missionary, Dr. Livingstone, survived in the deepest places of Africa through cutting blood covenants with different strong tribes. I will give you more details on this later.

You have probably heard the phrase "blood brothers." A few decades ago—before the onset of AIDS and Ebola—youngsters innocently poked the end of their fingertips to produce a drop of blood that they then "mixed" with a friend's blood, making them blood brothers or sisters. It all comes from the same source, whether it is taken seriously by a tribe or a group of adults or it is kids playing.

Are there any other examples of blood covenants today? Yes, let me give you one example.

One of the places we find blood covenants today is within the Italian and Chinese Mafia groups in the United States. It is called "omertá" and is a blood oath, a code of silence to never reveal the "family's" activities to the authorities.

This has caused the police a lot of problems when it comes to bringing people to justice.

In October 2014, the mafia "family" Cosa Nostra was taken down because after more than a 100 years of protection by the omertá. Someone has spoken, and 127 mobsters were arrested largely on the strength of informants.[1] It will be interesting to see what happens to these informants. It depends on what they agreed to when they took the blood oath.

You see, the blood covenant is such a powerful covenant, that it still produces what is agreed upon between the parties. It is working spiritually and practically!

Blood covenants are so powerful that they work both spiritually and practically.

An example of this: A CIA operative went to work undercover with the Mafia. He could not be accepted into the family without cutting a blood covenant with them. They would mix some of his blood and some of the blood of a member of the family in a cup of water and they would both drink from it and utter a curse. If he betrayed the family he would die a horrible death of the throat and tongue. Obviously this agent reported back to the CIA with everything he found out, ant the family was arrested, tried and punished. What happened to the agent? He got cancer of the throat that spread to the tongue and it resulted in his death.[2] That actually happened!

People who have gone to the police with information about the group have died of throat cancer. A blood covenant is a very serious matter! Another example is Tommaso Buscetta from the Italian mafia. He was the first mafia boss to turn informant, and he died from cancer.[3]

Some of today's inner-city gangs require new members to shed blood—their own or another's blood—as a sign of loyalty. Even some "hazing" rituals on college and university campuses involve bloodshed as part of a commitment on behalf of the fraternity and an individual.

We will examine the nine Hebrew rituals in the following chapter. These form the basis for the solid foundation we are laying for our lives of abundance. Then we will see why it is so important to understand how godly covenants work today.

Endnotes

1. http://www.dailymaverick.co.za/article/2011-01-22-the-new-york-mafias-very-bad-day-at-work/#.VEpVSkuYWb8 accessed 22 October 2014.

2. A.B. Lever, *And God said...* (Xulon Press, 2007). Chapter 17 "The Redemption Plan."

3. http://elpais.com/diario/2000/04/0 internacional/954885611_850215. html, accessed 22 October 2014; http://www.nytimes. com/2000/04/06/world/tommaso-buscetta-71-dies-first-italian-mafia-informer.html; accessed 22 October 2014.

Chapter Three

The Nine Hebrew Rituals

Now we will examine the nine traditional rituals and symbolism of a Hebrew blood covenant.

People in biblical times knew exactly what a blood covenant was all about, so there was no need to explain it fully to them. Consequently, the only place it is clearly shown in the Word of God is in Genesis 15, where we find the making of the covenant between God and Abraham.

After these things the word of the Lord came to Abram in a vision, saying, "Do not be afraid, Abram. I am your shield, your exceedingly great reward." ...And it came to pass, when the sun went down and it was dark, that behold, there appeared a smoking oven and a burning torch that passed between those pieces. On the same day the Lord made a covenant with Abram...

Genesis 15:1,17-18

Today, very few Christians understand the ritual revealed in Genesis 15:9-17 and how it was executed, but I believe it is extremely critical for God's children to recognize its importance so we can understand the Word of God. This blood covenant is what gave Jesus the right to act on our behalf. As we examine the different, most common rituals of a Hebrew blood covenant, please keep Jesus in the back of your mind.

Typical Rituals of a Hebrew Blood Covenant

Ritual 1:
Shedding Blood from Pure Animals
(See Genesis 15:9-10.)

It was necessary to prepare pure animals in a special way. They were cut in two halves, from the neck down to the tail. This was the sacrificial cutting of pure animals such as the three-year-old heifer, three-year-old female goat, three-year-old ram, turtledove, and young pigeon mentioned in Genesis 15:9.

The two halves, each part with two legs, were then placed back-to-back with the legs pointing outward, and leaving a space to walk between the two animal parts, making a *horizontal figure eight.* The pure birds, like the dove were not cut like this, but sacrificially killed and placed in the same pattern. Much blood was shed in this preparation.

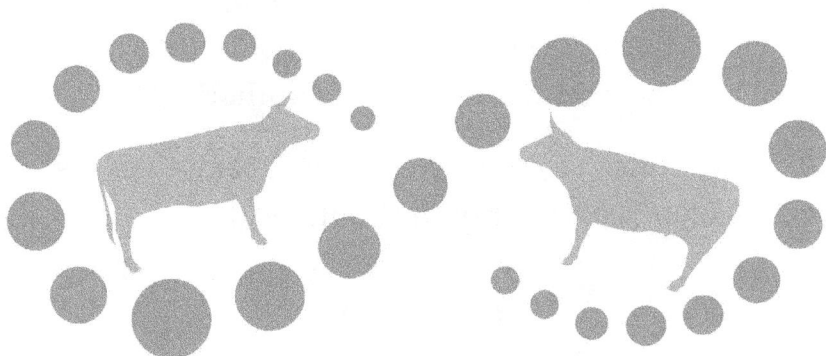

The horizontal figure eight, or two rings side by side and connected, is the symbol of eternity. The two parties making the covenant then placed themselves back-to-back in the center of the figure eight, where the two circles meet, between all the bloody animals. They started out as two individuals, back-to-back, and they each walked his half, one circle of the figure eight, meeting again in the middle face-to-face.

Now they started the process of becoming one, and blood covenant friends.

Ritual 2:
Mingling Blood

Standing face-to-face in the middle after each having walked his circle of the eternal symbol eight, *they lifted their right hand and made a cut until blood was flowing in the hand or the wrist.*

Then they grabbed each other's right hand and joined the open cuts, "blending" their blood.

This signified that they had stopped being two individuals *and were now in the process of becoming one man.* The right hand signifies the hand of authority.

The two men would look upon themselves as one person—blood covenant friends unto death.

Ritual 3:
Exchanging the Mantle
(See 1 Kings 19:16-19.)

A man's cloak signified the person himself. Exchanging a cloak, or mantle, meant: *"I give you all that I am and all that I have,* and you give me all that *you are* and all that *you have."*

We find stories of exchanging mantles throughout the Bible. Did you know what it meant? First Kings 19:16-19 gives us an excellent example.

Elijah the prophet was told by God to anoint Elisha in his place. When Elijah threw his mantle onto Elisha, the young man, Elisha immediately understood what it meant. He sacrificed the pair of oxen he was plowing with, using the yoke of wood to burn it. Animals were cut, blood shed, sacrificed, and burned—all tokens of a "hidden in plain sight" blood covenant.

"I give you all that I am and all the I have ... you give me all that you are and all that you have."

Elisha understood that *all that Elijah was and **all** he had, his calling and his anointing as a prophet, were given to him in that moment!* He stood up from the sacrifice and immediately left his old life as a rich heir, to follow and serve Elijah for the rest of his life.

When God later took Elijah up to heaven before the eyes of Elisha, *Elijah's mantle* fell down to Elisha, who took it and started out in his ministry as a prophet with the same, but double anointing of Elijah.

After we examine all nine rituals, I encourage you to read the Bible stories referred to in this chapter to see what more there is to discover through the Holy Spirit's guidance.

Ritual 4:
Exchange of Belts/Girdles
(See First Samuel 18:4.)

The men in biblical times did not use belts to keep up their trousers.

They used girdles around their waist, which were also used to carry swords, knives, etc. This exchange then clearly signifies *protection*, saying, "I will defend you until death, and anyone who attacks you, is attacking me. I will give my very life for you if necessary."

Ritual 5:
Name Exchanges

When the blood was mixed, their names were changed as well. An example from the Bible is found in Genesis 17:5 when Jehovah gave Abram the letters "ah," and changed his name to Abraham. This also changed the significance of his name to "father of multitudes." God changed Abraham's wife's name from Sarai to Sarah, exchanging an "i" for an "h."

In many countries in the world, still today, when a woman marries, she exchanges her last name for her husband's last name. Marriage as an institution is a blood covenant from the beginning. The norm from old was that two virgins married and blood was shed the first time they were intimately together. The Bible and our marriage rituals still say that the man and woman who were two individuals become *one flesh* through marriage.

Blood covenant talk! When two people marry, God says rightly in His Word that marriage is unbreakable and a covenant forever.

The custom today of changing husbands and wives and even partners outside of marriage, has a lot of spiritual implications and many times results in real burdens for all the persons involved, including children. I will explain this in more detail in Chapter 11.

The exchange of names signifies that two people are part of each other's life.

Ritual 6:
Treatment of the Cut

To prevent the scar from the cutting of the blood covenant to disappear, they would treat the wounds with ashes or paint. It was important to have proof of the blood covenant. In this way they would always be able to show proof of the Blood Covenant and that they had a blood covenant friend—a friend who was willing to protect them with his life.

Perhaps you have heard about "Stanley and Livingstone." Dr. David Livingstone was a Scottish missionary doctor committed to do God's will in Africa. When Livingstone went missing, newspaper reporter Henry Stanley was sent to find him, and upon doing so, uttered the well-known greeting, "Doctor Livingstone, I presume?"

None of the missionaries up to this point in the mid-1840s had been able to survive the fierce tribes who killed anyone stepping into their territory. Dr. Livingstone set out to find the source of the Nile and started penetrating uncharted territories of Africa. Other people who had tried this had died either from illnesses or from the hostile tribes.

I have read that Dr. Livingstone learned about blood covenants, which kept him safe. He wanted protection; they probably got gifts and other things from Europe. Dr. Livingstone entered into blood covenants with at least 50 tribes; when someone attacked him, all he had to do was show his scars of blood covenants and the attacker stopped. The tribes knew that if they harmed this man, they would have all the tribes he had a covenant with coming after them. Nobody dared harm him—he had way too many powerful friends. He and his explorer partner Henry Stanley later testified that they had never seen a blood covenant broken.[2]

Ritual 7:
Proclamation in Front of Witnesses

Every blood covenant has blessings and curses. It has blessings for fulfilling the covenant and curses for breaking the covenant.

These blessings and curses were proclaimed with a loud voice in front of witnesses. For instance: *"If I die, you will take care of my children and family. From this day on you are responsible for me. If I have a problem, I do not need to ask for your help, I will give you my problems and expect you to solve them. All you have is mine and all I have is yours!"*

If a man broke a blood covenant, he had signed his own death sentence. It was so shameful to break the covenant bond, which violated the honor of his name and his family's name, that his own family would personally seek to kill him. Breaking a blood covenant meant total loss of honor for him and his family.

Are you getting more curious about how Jesus had the right to take our sins and curses? He who was totally innocent? Keep reading, my friend.

Ritual 8:
Blood Covenant Meal and Gifts

There was always a meal following the cutting of a blood covenant. To eat together was very significant and serious. The person did not invite just anyone to eat in his home, because that meant that he invited him as a *friend* and he might stay in your house for quite a while—which was the custom back in biblical days.

The blood covenant meal consisted of at least bread, wine, and salt.

The salt was to preserve (take care of), the bread was and still is a symbol of the human body, and the wine was and is still the symbol of the blood and life.

The two blood covenant friends would say something like: *"I break this bread that symbolizes my body and give it to you, and I give you this wine as a symbol of my life blood, a life that now belongs to you forever."*

Those in covenant together share one body— one flesh.

Sound familiar?

The two blood covenant friends were now one body—one flesh.

Exchange of Gifts

The two parties gave each other gifts, often made of gold and silver, confirming the covenant.

A typical gift was a gold or silver ring, representing the eternal covenant of friendship, without beginning or end, to wear in the nose or on the finger. (Hippies and punks in the 1960s didn't invent nose rings, they were worn thousands of years ago.)

Ritual 9:
Build an Altar

(See Genesis 21:33.)

After everything was said and done, the two parties and their families built an altar as a memorial of the blood covenant just having been cut. It could be an altar of stones sprinkled with blood from the sacrifices, or *they might plant a tree and sprinkle it with blood.*

The tree is a symbol of a human all through the Bible. Through my Bible studies and the Holy Spirit's teaching, I have found that the main rule of interpretation of God's Word is that the Bible always interprets the Bible. If you find a symbol for one thing in the book of Genesis, or in two or three places, it will have the same meaning throughout the Bible. For example, *stars* is used for a *multitude* (see Deuteronomy 1:10, 10:22; Genesis 15:5; Nehemiah 9:23). *Sand* is used for *innumerable* (see Joshua 11:4; Judges 7:12; First Samuel 13:5; First Kings 4:29; Psalm 139:18).

The Bible always interprets the Bible.

This last ritual was the proclamation of two humans cutting a blood covenant, the sprinkling of the blood signifying that they were willing to commit their lives to and for each other. From now on they call themselves friends.

Are you excited about this new revelation? I'm excited to share with you the importance of blood covenants—and how they lead to your personal success contract.

We have now looked at the nine common rituals of the Hebrew blood covenant. You may be starting to see our Lord Jesus, and with the help of the Holy Spirit and a bit more explanation, you will receive this revelation even more clearly.

Next we will explore more deeply the blood covenant between God and Abram. Let's go!

Endnotes

1. Sten Nilson, *Blodspakten* (The Blood Covenant).
2. Cathy Jackson, *A Standing Invitation: Your Key to the Heart of God* (Xulon Press, 2010).

The Success Contract

Chapter Four

The Covenant Between God and Abraham

In Genesis 12:1-3 we first hear about a covenant between God and Abram. I believe there must have been a powerful incident and call from God that convinced Abram and gave him the faith he needed to leave his very comfortable life and his family.

Abram was living in a prosperous city, Ur in Chaldea, which was located in heathen Babylonia. Chaldea contained riches beyond imagination, and Ur was the wealthiest of the cities. Today Ur is in Iraq, about 160 kilometers (about 100 miles) northwest of the Kuwait border. In Abram's time, archaeologists estimate that there were about 24,000 people living in Ur. Ur was a highly advanced culture with the common district filled with schools, libraries, and marketplaces, and many people were very wealthy.

The Success Contract

Abram was a member of a wealthy family; his father was a jeweler who made and sold idols of gold and silver. Abram and his family probably lived, as was normal in Ur, in a two or three story house with inside plumbing and bathrooms, surrounded by lush gardens. Yet Abram went out from all this comfort into the desert to live in a tent!

We do not know what kind of godly encounter made him give it up and leave almost everything behind, but it must have been something very powerful! Abram must have met with God face-to-face or at least in a way that totally shook him out of his comfort zone.

Abram took with him his wife Sarai, his father, his nephew, and many servants and animals. He left the city of Ur—and he did not even know where he was going.

I am eternally grateful for Abram's obedience and for God's provision of this man of faith who was part of His ultimate rescue plan for humankind. God spoke to all His Old Testament prophets with an audible voice. We see later that Abram was one of these prophets.

When we first meet Abram and his family, we see God entering into a covenant with him, giving several promises in Genesis 12:1-3:

> *Now the Lord had said to Abram: "Get out of your country, from your family and from your father's house, to a land that I will show you."*

The Covenant Between God And Abraham

"I will make you a great nation" (a people, multitudes).

Abram did not yet have any children. His wife, Sarai, was barren, so that seemed a bit difficult.

"I will bless you" (spiritually and naturally).

Later we will see an extension of this covenant when God cuts a blood covenant with Abram.

"I will make your name great" (exalt his name).

"You shall be a blessing" (for many others).

"I will bless those who bless you and curse those who curse you." (Israel, the descendants of Abraham today, still carry these two promises from God.)

According to the Word of God, we are all descendants from Abraham's loins. (The Jews as genuine children and the Gentiles as adopted children, with exactly the same rights.)

What God did with and for Abraham, He also did for all His children—including you!

Let us study the only place in the Bible that reveals some details about the blood covenant. We find this Abrahamic blood covenant in Genesis 15.

Abram is now about 99 years old, and the Bible says Sarai was past the age of childbearing. In Genesis 15:3-6 we find

Abraham complaining to God. He is now an old man and has lost all hope of having a child and seeing the promised multitude of people and heirs. Abram was ready to make Eliezer, a young man born in his house, his heir.

Abraham and God have the following conversation:

> *Then Abram said, "Look, You have given me no offspring; indeed one born in my house is my heir!"*
> ### Genesis 15:3

In other words, Abram was saying, God, You are a liar! You have NOT kept your promise from the covenant we made!

> *And behold, the word of the Lord came to him, saying, This one shall not be your heir, **but one who will come from your own body shall be your heir."***
> ### Genesis 15:4

Yes, right! Abram was 99 years old!

> *Then He brought him outside and said, "Look now toward heaven, and count the stars if you are able to number them." And He said to him, "So shall your descendants be."*
> ### Genesis 15:5

> *And he [Abram] believed in the Lord, and He [God] accounted it to him for righteousness.*
> ### Genesis 15:6

Then He said to him, "I am the Lord, who brought you out of Ur of the Chaldeans, to give you this land to inherit it."
Genesis 15:7

Now, this time, Abram wants a valid promise from God:

And he said, "Lord God, how shall I know that I will inherit it?"
Genesis 15:8

Good question, Abram! Now here comes the way God shows Abram that He will keep His promise. Let's see if you recognize what God is saying next.

*So He said to him, "Bring Me a three-year-old heifer, a three-year-old female goat, a three-year-old ram, a turtledove, and a young pigeon" Then he brought all these to Him **and cut them in two, down the middle, and placed each piece opposite the other; but he did not cut the birds in two.***
Genesis 15:9-10

We are talking "pure animals" here! Can you imagine how Abram was told to cut them? He cut them from the neck and down to the tail, making two equal pieces that were ready to be put into the horizontal figure eight.

The Bible is talking about a blood covenant, just about to take place between God and Abram.

*Now when the sun was going down, **a deep sleep fell upon Abram**; and behold, horror and great darkness fell upon him.*
Genesis 15:12

Abram was put aside; the Bible says he was in *a deep sleep*, but how would he later be able to explain all that happened? Abram was of course not sleeping. The word in Hebrew means "lethargy" or paralyzed. He was set into what is also known as a *trance*, the highest form of personal vision.

When you enter a trance, your physical body is in a paralyzed-like state, but you can clearly see, feel, and hear everything that is going on, as if you were looking at a movie.

While Abram, who represents humanity, was put aside, someone else was making a blood covenant on his behalf—and our behalf. These two people were cutting the blood covenant for Abram and us!

Let us look more closely at the key Scripture that leads us to the answer of the question: Why did Jesus Christ have the right to take our sins and curses upon Himself?

*And it came to pass, when the sun went down and it was dark, that behold, there appeared **a smoking oven and a burning torch that passed between those pieces.***
Genesis 15:17

What was happening here? What or who are the "smoking oven and the burning torch"? Definitely not Abram, as he was put aside unable to move a finger! Chapter 5 explores this mystery fully—you may be surprised by the revelations.

Chapter Five

The Bible Interprets the Bible

The Smoking Oven and Burning Torch

A s mentioned previously, if we find a word in the Bible that means something in Genesis, it will have the same meaning throughout the Bible. The symbolism in the Bible has the same meaning wherever we find it, in any of the 66 books.

We are now in Genesis 15:17 trying to find out who the Smoking Oven and the Burning Torch are.

Who Is the Smoking Oven?

If Bible interprets Bible, we find the "smoking oven" or furnace mentioned in several Old Testament Scripture passages:

The Success Contract

*Now Mount Sinai was completely in smoke, because the Lord [Jehovah] descended upon it in fire. Its smoke ascended **like the smoke of a furnace,** and the whole mountain quaked greatly.*
Exodus 19:18

*Then he looked toward Sodom and Gomorrah, and toward all the land of the plain; and he saw, and behold, the smoke of the land which went up **like the smoke of a furnace** (Father God coming down in judgment).*
Genesis 19:28

And the Lord **[Jehovah] said to Moses, "Behold, I come to you in the thick cloud,** *that the people may hear when I speak with you, and believe you forever." So Moses told the words of the people to the Lord.*
Exodus 19:9

Then the Lord said to Moses, "Go to the people and consecrate them today and tomorrow, and let them wash their clothes. And let them be ready for the third day. For on the third day the Lord [Jehovah] will come down upon Mount Sinai in the sight of all the people.

...So Moses went down from the mountain to the people and sanctified the people, and they washed

their clothes. And he said to the people, "Be ready for the third day; do not come near your wives"
Exodus 19:10-15

*Then it came to pass on the third day, in the morning, that there were **thunderings and lightnings, and a thick cloud on the mountain; and the sound of the trumpet was very loud,** so that all the people who were in the camp trembled.*
Exodus 19:16

*Now all the people witnessed the thunderings, the lightning flashes, the sound of the trumpet, **and the mountain smoking;** and when the people saw it, they trembled and stood afar off.*
Exodus 20:18

In my distress I called upon the Lord [Jehovah], and cried out to my God; He heard my voice from His temple, and my cry entered His ears. Then the earth shook and trembled; the foundations of heaven quaked and were shaken, because He was angry.
2 Samuel 22:7-8

***Smoke went up from His nostrils, and devouring fire from His mouth;** coals were kindled by it.*
2 Samuel 22:9

He bowed the heavens also, and came down with darkness under His feet. He rode upon a cherub, and flew; and He was seen upon the wings of the wind.
2 Samuel 22:10

He made darkness canopies around Him, dark waters and thick clouds of the skies.
2 Samuel 22:12

*He shall cross over to his stronghold for fear, and his princes shall be afraid of the banner, says the **Lord** [Jehovah], **whose fire is in Zion and whose furnace is in Jerusalem.***
Isaiah 31:9

From these passages from God's Word, we can accurately conclude that the Smoking Oven (Furnace) is referring to Jehovah, God the Father!

Who Is the Burning Torch?

Now let's examine passages from the Bible that reveal who is the Burning Torch.

*And the Angel of the Lord [Jehovah] appeared to him in **a flame of fire** from the midst of a bush. So he looked, and behold, the bush was burning with fire, but the bush was not consumed.*
Exodus 3:2

In several Bible translations we find the phrase, "Angel of the Lord." Angel written with a capital "A" indicates Jesus, our Lord. When we find "angel" with small "a" it indicates normal angels. So Exodus 3:2 is referring to the Lord Jesus; He is also referred to as a "flame of fire" (torch).

*So **the Light of Israel** will be for a fire, **and his Holy One for a flame;** it will burn and devour his thorns and his briers in one day.*

Isaiah 10:17

*In the beginning was the Word, and **the Word was with God**, and the Word was God. He was in the beginning with God. All things were made through Him, and without Him nothing was made that was made.*

John 1:1-3

In Him was life, and the life was the light of men.

John 1:4

The Word coming alive as Light was and is the Lord Jesus.

*"Is not **My word like a fire?"** says the Lord, "And like a hammer that breaks the rock in pieces?"*

Jeremiah 23:29

*Then Jesus spoke to them again, saying, **"I am the light of the world. He who follows Me shall not walk in darkness, but have the light of life."***

John 8:12

So who is the Burning Torch, the Light of the World, and the Flaming Fire? It is obviously our Lord Jesus Christ!

The blood covenant cut in Genesis 15:17, about 4,000 years ago, was made between God the Father and God the Son.

Abram, representing the people of Israel—and later you and me and all believers—was put aside, being totally unable to move.

Why did God choose this process? It is simple and yet difficult to understand.

God the Father is the Ultimate Leader who takes complete responsibility for His creation. When His creation, humanity, failed and fell into sin, the whole perfect plan of God for all of His children was thwarted. God, as the Good Leader of us all, takes the responsibility to correct humankind's mistake.

Only One Way

There was only *one way* God could solve this problem. He had to correct the man-made error and reconcile humankind to God. To put humankind back into the same position they had before the fall into sin in the Garden, God had to give His Son the right to take humanity's place in the righteous judgment of God of all humans.

When we examined the different rituals and agreements of the Hebrew blood covenant earlier, we understood that the two parties start out as two independent people. Then after walking the eternal eight and cutting the covenant, they become one person.

Now in Genesis 12:1-3, God makes the first covenant with promises to Abram, if he is faithful and obedient. Not only would God bless him abundantly, but He would also make him a blessing. Even those who bless Abram would be blessed, and those who curse him would be cursed.

Three chapters and many years later, God cuts this covenant in blood, making it the strongest and most powerful agreement He could possibly make. Abram was then convinced that he, himself, would have his own heir and son. I am sure he also expected to be part of walking the eternal figure eight with God, being physically part of the procedure.

Not so!

After preparing all the animals, cutting them sacrificially correctly, God says, *"That's it Abram, now I will put you into a trance, so you, being a man, cannot mess up what I am doing again."*

Abram could not move, only watch and hear (see Genesis 15:12).

From this moment on Abram knew that he would have a son of his own. It did not matter that he was almost 100 years old and that his wife, Sarai, was way beyond the years of childbearing. He knew that God had made a blood covenant with him, and then the matter was settled forever, even if he was 99 and Sarai was 90 years old.

Have you ever heard of a woman conceiving and birthing a child at the age of 90? Me neither. That was definitely a "God thing!"

We see how God renews and extends His covenant promises and adds to them that Abram's descendants will inherit Canaan, the Promised Land (see Genesis 17:8-9). God changes Abram's name to Abraham, meaning "the father of multitudes" and promises him a son within one year (see Genesis 17:5-6). That promise was fulfilled to the letter. In one year, Abraham, being 100 years old, welcomed his first legitimately born son, Isaac (see Genesis 17:19-21.

God's Rescue Plan

Humankind was disconnected from God after sinning. He had broken a covenant that was supposed to be a complete success contract from God and was accordingly judged to die apart from God and go to hell. *But God in His mercy,* arranged for humankind's protection by once a year allowing the high priest to offer blood on behalf of the people by sacrificing animals. This sacrifice was only an annual cover, nothing lasting or changing.

God's rescue plan began with the blood covenant with Abram. God allowed the Lord Jesus to take humankind's place in the ritual, representing all people. Humanity and Jesus became one person. When God became One with His Son, that meant He could later

God's rescue plan for us began with His blood covenant with Abram.

use His Son as a substitute for humanity on the cross, as Jesus and humankind were *one!*

How?

Melchizedek and Abram

If we go one chapter back to Genesis 14:14-24, it tells the story of when the family and property of Abram and Lot were robbed by some enemy kings. The very interesting point here is the section that talks about Melchizedek, his name meaning "King of Righteousness," representing God most High and Abram's covenant partner. Abram and several hundred of his servants had persecuted these evil kings and regained everything they had stolen.

> *Now when Abram heard that his brother was taken captive, he armed his three hundred and eighteen trained servants who were born in his own house, and went in pursuit as far as Dan. He divided his forces against them by night, and he and his servants attacked them and pursued them as far as Hobah, which is north of Damascus. So he brought back all the goods, and also brought back his brother Lot and his goods, as well as the women and the people.*
>
> *And the king of Sodom went out to meet him at the Valley of Shaveh (that is, the King's Valley), after his*

return from the defeat of Chedorlaomer and the kings who were with him.

Then Melchizedek king of Salem brought out bread and wine; *he was the priest of God Most High. And he blessed him and said: "Blessed be Abram of God Most High, Possessor of heaven and earth; and blessed be God Most High, who has delivered your enemies into your hand." And he gave him a tithe of all.*

Now the king of Sodom said to Abram, "Give me the persons, and take the goods for yourself." But Abram said to the king of Sodom, "I have raised my hand to the Lord, God Most High, the Possessor of heaven and earth, that I will take nothing, from a thread to a sandal strap, and that I will not take anything that is yours, lest you should say, 'I have made Abram rich'— except only what the young men have eaten, and the portion of the men who went with me: Aner, Eshcol, and Mamre; let them take their portion."

Two things reveal the blood covenant here, and we need to study this Scripture passage to see who was Melchizedek.

First they shared a covenant meal together—Abram and the King of Righteousness, or Melchizedek, representing God Most High. Then Abram gave him a covenant gift, later known as the tithe or 10 percent of everything he had gained of spoil.

Genesis chapter 14 is very significant because it comes just before God makes the other blood covenant in Genesis 15:17, where it is much more clear what is happening.

The most important thing here is to understand who Melchizedek is. To find out for sure, and because the Bible says by two witnesses a thing is true, go with me to the book of Hebrews:

> *For this Melchizedek, king of Salem, priest of the Most High God, who met Abraham returning from the slaughter of the kings and blessed him, to whom also Abraham gave a tenth part of all, first being translated "king of righteousness," and then also king of Salem, meaning "king of peace," without father, without mother, without genealogy, having neither beginning of days nor end of life, but made like the Son of God, remains a priest continually. Now consider how great this man was, to whom even the patriarch Abraham gave a tenth of the spoils.*
>
> ### Hebrews 7:1-4

Melchizedek is the Lord Jesus. When Jesus and Abram cut a blood covenant in Genesis 14, they went from being two individuals to become *one* person. Covenant friends and all Jesus had was Abram's and all Abram had belonged to Jesus.

From then on either one of them had the right to be the part of the blood covenant cut in Genesis 15:17, where you see the Burning Torch (Jesus) and the Smoking Oven (Father God) cutting a blood covenant on behalf of humanity. Jesus was doing it, putting Abram (humanity) to the side in a trance, paralyzed, but awake.

The blood covenant in Genesis 14 already gave our Lord Jesus the right to take the place of humanity on the cross, punishing Him for our sins and taking our sicknesses and curses. All humanity had, all the bad stuff, was already His by covenant.

Jesus Christ had two times proved His right to go to the cross and take our punishment for us.

Circumcision

Circumcision is a blood covenant between God and every Jew, every male child (see Genesis 17:10-12). God also institutes circumcision, cutting of the foreskin of all males coming from Abraham and his flock, as a sign of their blood covenant promises with God. They cut this covenant when the baby boy is exactly eight days old because that is when the healing process goes especially fast, preordained by God.

Abraham and his son's descendants will be a covenant people from now on. The people coming out of the "loins of Abraham" are Israel. We as Christians and believers are adopted as children with the same rights. The Jews are still practicing circumcision today, as do many Christians worldwide. We will later come back to the circumcision as part of the blood covenant.

The Sacrifice of Isaac

After waiting all his life for a son and heir, Abraham has to pass the most difficult test of faith in his whole life. God asked Abraham to sacrifice—kill—his only son, Isaac, that He had promised and given him. Isaac may have been in his teens, yet there is no indication that he ever doubted what his father Abraham was asked to do—amazing! In total obedience Abraham was willing to follow the Lord's instructions.

Then He said, "Take now your son, your only son Isaac, whom you love, and go to the land of Moriah, and offer him there as a burnt offering on one of the mountains of which I shall tell you."
Genesis 22:2

Abraham obeyed *immediately!*

Have you ever asked yourself, *How could God ask Abraham to do that—to sacrifice his only son he waited so long for? And how could Abraham obey?* Abraham could follow the Lord's instruction only because he knew that God could *not break* His blood covenant. Even if Abraham did kill Isaac, God would have revived him! Abraham knew that the incredible power of the blood covenant would work—without any doubt at all.

God tested the obedience and willingness of His servant and friend Abraham to sacrifice the best he had. God rescued Isaac by providing an animal as the sacrifice, just as Abraham lifted the knife to kill Isaac.

Abraham passed the test! Isaac also passed the test of being an obedient son all the way unto death.

This is a fantastic example of what Father God and Jesus His Son would do about 2,000 years later in the eternal new blood covenant made on the cross!

We need to say, "THANK YOU, ABRAHAM!"

Chapter Six

Jesus Christ and the Blood Covenant Rituals

L et's reexamine the nine rituals of the Hebrew blood covenant—but this time focusing on the Lord Jesus. Let's see and understand what He has really done for you and me.

Jesus and the Rituals

Ritual 1
Shedding Pure Blood

The two parties met together and agreed on their conditions for an eternal new friendship and commitment. The pure animals were cut and laid on the ground, forming a horizontal figure eight, leaving a walking space between the pieces.

Jesus, the Burning Torch, walked the blood covenant on our behalf, together with our Father God, the Smoking Oven (see Genesis 15:17).

Jesus took our place as a substitute way back in Old Testament times, more than 2,000 years before He would be born into a human body and walk here on earth.

In the New Testament, Jesus took again, once and for all, our place as an innocent Lamb, the perfect and eternal Sacrifice, as our blood covenant partner on the cross.

Ritual 2
Mingling Blood

Two men lifted their right hands and cut the wrist or hand until blood flowed.

Our Lord Jesus was crucified; His wrists were nailed to the cross with nails thicker than your largest finger—pierced until blood flowed. (We will study the significance of crucifixion as another foundational stone in Chapter 8.)

Ritual 3
Exchanging the Mantel

The two parties exchanged their mantels. The mantel of a person signified "All that I am and all that I have I will give to you."

Our Lord Jesus was crucified naked. It was a very shameful position for any person, so also for our Lord Jesus.

They took away His "mantel," or clothing, that was made out of one piece of linen. (Symbolizing purity, and worth much money.)

The soldiers who crucified Jesus cast lots for Jesus' mantel because it was so expensive! His mantel was *all* that He was and *all* He had—and was given to the worst sinners of that time, the Roman soldiers, representing you and me before the Lord saved us!

It is hard for mere humans to fathom such an amazing act of love, mercy, and compassion. As you are reading, I pray that you will allow the Holy Spirit to reveal to you in prayer what was actually exchanged for you on the cross that day.

> **You have inherited authority from your Lord and Savior.**

You have inherited authority from your Lord and Savior—unlimited authority through the words you speak and things you do. You have *all* that He is and *all* that He has available to you on certain conditions. The blood covenant means that everything you have is His and everything He has is yours *as long as **you** stay in the covenant.*

In Ephesians 1:19-23 we read:

> *And what is the exceeding greatness of His power toward us who believe, according to the working of His mighty power which He worked in Christ when He raised Him*

*from the dead and seated Him at His right hand in the
heavenly places, far above all principality and power
and might and dominion, and every name that is
named, not only in this age but also in that which is to
come. And He put all things under His feet, and gave
Him to be head over all things to the church, which
is His body, the fullness of Him who fills all in all.*

The power in Christ is in you *as long as you stay connected
to Him, the Head.*

Galatians 2:20 says:

*I have been crucified with Christ; it is no longer I
who live, but Christ lives in me; and the life which
I now live in the flesh I live by faith in the Son of
God, who loved me and gave Himself for me.*

Sin is the main thing that will keep us from walking in
the promises. Galatians 5:19-20 says:

*Now the works of the flesh are evident, which are:
adultery, fornication, uncleanness, lewdness, idolatry,
sorcery, hatred, contentions, jealousies, outbursts
of wrath, selfish ambitions, dissensions, heresies,
envy, murders, drunkenness, revelries, and the
like; of which I tell you beforehand, just as I also*

*told you in time past, that **those who practice such things will not inherit the kingdom of God.***

And in Romans 6:1-2 we find:

What shall we say then? Shall we continue in sin that grace may abound? Certainly not! How shall we who died to sin live any longer in it?

Ritual 4
Exchange of Girdles/Belts

The two parties exchanged girdles, or belts—the broad piece of cloth tied around their waists. As Hebrew men did not wear trousers with pockets, this wide belt was used to carry their swords and knives. It was a girdle of defense.

Before He was crucified, our Lord Jesus had already been deprived of that belt by the soldiers who beat Him and crucified Him. Again symbolizing His protection of sinners—you and me, and all of humankind.

Remember, the Bible says that Jesus could have stopped the crucifixion process at *any time* if He had wanted to. He had legions (thousands) of angels ready to serve Him, doing exactly what He ordered! If He had wanted to back out of God's plan to be our substitute, He could have done so.

But he did not do that. Just like His forefather Isaac (who willingly lay on the altar under the knife of his father

Abraham), our Lord was led like a Lamb to be slaughtered, willingly. We are forever grateful for His decision that day! His decision saved our eternal life and reconciled us to our Father God.

Jesus exchanged his belt of defense for us and instead of being destined for hell, *we are now on our way to heaven!*

Ritual 5
Name Exchanges

The two parties exchanged names. The norm was to exchange part of names or add the other person's name.

Jesus gave us His whole name! Our Lord Jesus is such a generous Lord that after being crucified and resurrected, He allowed us to *ask in His name!* He said to His disciples:

> *And whatever you ask in **My name**, that I will do, that the Father may be glorified in the Son. If you ask anything in My name, I will do it.*

John 14:13-14

Did Jesus only give us a letter or two of His name? No, He did not. He is so extremely good and generous that He gave us His whole name—the name of Jesus. He said that whatever we ask the Father in His name—Jesus—the Father will give it to us.

Now you know where the power in using the name of Jesus comes from—again, the blood covenant. It is unbreakable, if He said it, He will do it, unless we hinder things ourselves.

Ritual 6
Treatment of the Cut

The two people treated the cuts on their wrists or hands with ashes or paint to prevent the scars from disappearing.

Our Lord Jesus had huge nails plunged through His wrists, making holes and scars that will never disappear. People who have seen Him in visions over the years have all noticed the marks He still has from the crucifixion.

Ritual 7
Proclamation in Front of Witnesses

The two parties proclaimed with a loud voice in front of witnesses the promises of their agreement and eternal covenant.

Like I mentioned before, in those days they seldom used written agreements to seal business deals. Their name and testimony was the guarantee, and used witnesses to validate the deal or agreement.

Today this proclamation is called salvation or being born again. Our Lord Jesus gave us salvation through His sacrifice on the cross. We are completely reconciled with the Father through taking part in their blood covenant. How? Through believing and proclaiming.

The Success Contract

When a person gets saved today, being born again and born into the blood covenant through the blood of Christ, the person prays the prayer of faith and commitment in front of witnesses in the church, or elsewhere.

> *But what does it say? "The word is near you, in your mouth and in your heart" (that is, the word of faith which we preach): That if you confess with your mouth the Lord Jesus and believe in your heart that God has raised Him from the dead, you will be saved. For with the heart one believes unto righteousness, and **with the mouth confession is made unto salvation."***

> **Romans 10:8-10**

As this blood covenant is eternal and there is no distance in the spiritual realm, the following takes place in the spiritual realm when we agree to be part of God's family and pray the prayer of faith. The prayer can be something as simple as:

Lord Jesus, I need You. I open the door to my life for You, and I receive You as my Lord and Savior. Thank You for forgiving me of my sins by taking them on the cross for me.

I receive the blood covenant that You made and enter into it with You. Lord, take all I am and all I have. In Jesus' name, amen.

We say *yes* to receive Jesus Christ as our Lord and Savior.

Jesus Christ and the Blood Covenant Rituals

The Holy Spirit "cuts," taking out our human spirit with all its filth and sin, nails it to the cross (in the spirit) and *exchanges* it with a new Spirit—the Spirit of Jesus.

The Bible says that we are now a new creation, everything old has passed away, and everything is totally new.

Therefore, if anyone is in Christ, he is a new creation; old things have passed away; behold, all things have become new.

2 Corinthians 5:17

The exchange was done already more than 2,000 years ago on the cross when *the Lord Jesus made ready His part of the blood covenant,* giving *all* that He was and *all* that He had. He became our rightful substitute according to the "Old Blood Covenant" with Abraham. He is just waiting for you and me to do our part and enter into the "New Blood Covenant" with Him and the Father.

He had the right to take our place on the cross, bearing all our sins and taking all our curses and sicknesses (which are curses) on His body, because He was and is the pure Lamb of God, slain in our place. He did this so we could be free, even though He Himself was blameless and sinless!

The Bible says the only way to be part of this blood covenant is through Jesus Christ, through inviting Him into our lives as our Lord and Savior, proclaiming and praying the prayer of faith. Jesus is the *only* "Door" to enter in to God, being reconciled with the Father and becoming His child and heir. AMEN!

Ritual 8
Blood Covenant Meal and Gifts

When the two people had finished all the rituals and proclamations that were necessary, they shared a meal. The meal always consisted of at least *salt, bread, and wine.*

Our Lord Jesus initiated in John 13, something we today call "The Lord's Supper" or "Communion," consisting of eating bread and drinking wine (or grape juice) during a normal church service.

In 1 Corinthians 11:23-26, the apostle Paul refers to what the Lord was saying in Luke 22:15-20:

*For I received from the Lord that which I also delivered to you: that the Lord Jesus on the same night in which He was betrayed took bread; and when He had given thanks, He broke it and said, **"Take, eat; this is My body which is broken for you; do this in remembrance of Me."***

*In the same manner He also took the cup after supper, saying, **"This cup is the new covenant in My blood. This do, as often as you drink it, in remembrance of Me."***

For as often as you eat this bread and drink this cup, you proclaim the Lord's death till He comes.

The salt in the Hebrew blood covenant meal was a symbol of preservation of fresh food. Spiritually it meant preservation of the covenant and the promises that were made. Most Christian services do not use salt specifically in their covenant meal, the Lord's Supper, but there is salt within the bread that is broken and eaten in remembrance of Him. In Matthew 5:13, Jesus called believers "the salt of the earth."

The Lord told us to remember Him until He comes again, taking the bread as a symbol of His body broken for us and the wine as a symbol of His blood shared for us. It is a memorial, a tribute to the Lamb of God.

The covenant meal was and is significant and seals the agreement between the two parties—who now call themselves friends. When the Bible talks about friends, in the majority of places it refers to blood covenant friends, which has much more serious implications than today's reference to friends who hang out after a movie, watch a game, or have coffee together.

A blood covenant friend could come to your house when he wanted and eat your food, sharing your meals as long as he wanted. Basically he could stay with you in your house with your family for a couple of months at a time! Now you understand why the apostle Paul warns the Corinthians about continuous fellowship with the sinners among them who were not willing to repent and change.

Paul says, "Do not even *eat* with such a person." What Paul is really saying is do not have communion—eating and spending time with a sinner in your house, permitting him to influence your household for a long period of time!

If you do not understand the implications of a *blood covenant friend* eating and staying in your house, you might judge Paul for being too strict with the Corinthians. Should we not eat with sinners? Of course we should. Even Jesus ate with sinners, telling us this is why He came—to save sinners. Jesus spent more time with sinners than any of us, but He did not *live* with them, like He lived with His friends, the apostles.

We must take seriously our spiritual covenant—as sin is very contagious. We need to be very careful about whom we choose as close friends and companions. Are they people we can grow together with spiritually—or people who will influence us with their bad habits, like criticism, gossip, etc.

Just before going to the Cross, our Lord says:

> *No longer do I call you servants, for a servant does not know what his master is doing;* **but I have called you friends**, *for all things that I heard from My Father I have made known to you. You did not choose Me, but I chose you and appointed you that you should go and bear fruit, and that your fruit should remain, that* **whatever you ask the Father in My name He may give you.**
>
> **John 15:15-16**

Gift Exchange

The two people in the blood covenant process exchanged gifts; for instance, gold or silver rings for the nose, ears, or fingers.

We use rings the same way today when couples exchange rings during a marriage ceremony. The wedding ring was not first used during a marriage ritual; rather the tradition came from the blood covenant ritual that is more than 4,000 years old. The wedding ring is actually a symbol of the blood covenant that marriage is between two people. Unfortunately, the majority of couples getting married today do not have a clue about the real significance of the rings they exchange.

The wedding ring began as a ring *cut* around the base of the left thumb to show everyone the covenant they had as spouses. This way it could not be taken off like today—marriage is for life.[1]

Ritual 9
Build an Altar

The two parties joined strengths and built an altar as a memorial of their blood covenant.

They either built an altar of stones or they planted a tree. They sprinkled blood on the tree to seal the covenant.

The Cross

Our Lord Jesus poured out His very own lifeblood on the tree of the cross, being sacrificed for us. That is why Christians always will remember the cross of Jesus and His sacrifice for us—as a memorial until He returns to take us home with Him.

Christ has redeemed us from the curse of the law,
having become a curse for us (for it is written,
"Cursed is everyone who hangs on a tree."
Galatians 3:13

The Tree

A tree in the Bible signifies a human being. As mentioned previously, the Bible interprets the Bible, so when we see a tree signifying a human being one or more places in the Bible, it will always mean a human being, unless it has a name, like a fig tree or an almond tree.

The following are a few Scriptures mentioning trees that symbolize humankind:

Blessed is the man [and woman] *who walks not in the*
counsel of the ungodly, nor stand in the path of sinners,
nor sits in the seat of the scornful; but his delight is in
the law of the Lord, and in His law he meditates day and
night. **He shall be like a tree planted by the rivers**

of water, that brings forth its fruit in its season, whose leaf also shall not wither; and whatever he does shall prosper.

Psalm 1:1-3

The tree mentioned in Psalm 1:3 represents humankind. And according to the Bible, by two or three witnesses a thing is true.

Additional Scriptures where trees symbolize humans:

*I have seen **the wicked** in great power, and spreading himself **like a native green tree.***

Psalm 37:35

***Like an apple tree** among the trees of the woods, **so is my beloved among the sons.** I sat down in his shade with great delight, and his fruit was sweet to my taste.*

Song of Solomon 2:3

*For **he shall be like a tree planted by the waters,** which spreads out its roots by the river, and will not fear when heat comes; but its leaf will be green, and will not be anxious in the year of drought, nor will cease from yielding fruit.*

Jeremiah 17:8

*Beware **of false prophets,** who come to you in sheep's clothing, but inwardly they are ravenous wolves. **You will know them by their fruits.** Do men gather grapes from* *thornbushes or figs from thistles? Even so,* ***every good tree*** ***bears good fruit, but a bad tree bears bad fruit.***

Matthew 7:15-17

Jesus hung on the tree of the cross, forever connected to humankind by torturous nails hammered through His wrists and feet into the tree.

The Very Special Acacia Tree

The cross of Jesus Christ was made of wood from the Acacia tree. Wood from the Acacia tree was used in the Ark of the Covenant and in the Holy of Holiest (see Exodus 35:24; Leviticus 16). The table of the showbread (see Exodus 25:23) and the other furniture in the Holy Place was also made of Acacia, first in the Tabernacle and later in the Temple in Jerusalem! (See also Exodus 25–37.)

There are many uses for all the different parts of the tree. Acacia wood is hard, dense, and strong, and very dark in color. The *wood* is used to make ships, flooring, furniture, jewelry, weapons, and toys. Its *roots* hinder the dryness of the deserts from expanding; it stops at the feet of this tree. The *trunk* produces Arabic gum used in medicine, adhesives and industrial products. The *seeds* can be eaten raw or ground for flavoring food. The *flowers* used to make perfume and the *fruit* is also used for medicine.

There is something else that is very special about the acacia tree that is unlike any other tree. Its cells divide in exactly the same way as the cells of a human! The Acacia tree has the same "DNA" as a human being, so to speak.[2]

The Nails

The tree is a symbol of humankind, so our Lord was nailed to the symbol of humanity, the wood of an Acacia tree. A tree that according to the Bible is holy. Huge nails joined Jesus to the tree (to humankind), *making us one with Him.* At the same time, His blood flowed out onto the tree as a seal of protection.

The nails were between 13-18 centimeters (5-7 inches) long and 1 centimeter (half inch) thick, normally handmade by the Romans. A nail connects two materials together; a friction works sideways to help hold the two pieces even tighter together. Jesus and the tree were stuck together like glue. He was and is a shield, a covering, receiving all the sins, pain, and curses into His own body, soul, and mind—for us.

With of the symbol of humankind and Jesus Christ glued together on the cross, a New Eternal Blood Covenant was made between God and humanity through the substitute, the Son. *He became one with us physically and spiritually.*

In the time of the crucifixion of Jesus, some people believed the nails had a medical function and gathered them as amulets (ornament thought to give protection against evil, danger, or disease). The nails were valuable, expensive, and therefore used multiple times in different crucifixions.

There is so much more power and delegated authority in the blood covenant than we see and understand at first glance. I encourage you to read the following verse from God's Word and take time to think about the meaning. If you are a believer who has received the Lord Jesus as your Lord and personal Savior, pray about what this truth mean to you.

> *For you did not receive the spirit of bondage again to fear, but you received the Spirit of adoption by whom we cry out, "Abba, Father." The Spirit Himself bears witness with our spirit that we are children of God, and if children, then heirs—heirs of God and joint heirs with Christ, if indeed we suffer with Him, that we may also be glorified together.*
> **Romans 8:15-17**

Being born again, you are now a friend with Jesus and a child adopted by God—you are a genuine heir in the Kingdom of God! All Jesus has and is belongs to you from the very second that you are saved!

Endnotes

1. Cathy Jackson, *A Standing Invitation*.
2. http://topicosculturales.blogspot.com.es/2007/07/significado-bblico-y-cientfico-de-la.html; accessed 23 October 2014.

Chapter Seven

Preparation for the Cross

Gethsemane

What happened at Gethsemane is another foundational stone to understanding the judgment of Jesus on our behalf.

The judgment did not start with the scourging or even with the crucifixion—it started the evening before. *A crucial battle was won by our Lord Jesus in the garden of Gethsemane.*

The fight He fought in the garden of Gethsemane was mental, spiritual, and emotional. Although He was God, He was in a human body and knew He was about to suffer an incredibly painful death, the crucifixion. Consequently, He went through a time of real and true agony. *If He had not overcome and been victorious in that personal fight with His flesh, we would never have had the opportunity to receive salvation and be reconciled with God.*

Remember, our Lord could have rescued Himself and abandoned God's plan for Him at any given time—if He had wanted. The Father had given Him a free will and He had to choose to go through with God's plan of sacrifice and redemption!

The following two scriptures show you the terrible agony and fight of our Lord. It helps to read these in context.

Luke is the author of the first passage. He was a physician and very detailed in his recordings of this event.

Coming out, He went to the Mount of Olives, as He was accustomed, and His disciples also followed Him. When He came to the place, He said to them, **"Pray that you may not enter into temptation."** *And He was withdrawn from them about a stone's throw, and He knelt down and prayed, saying,* **"Father, if it is Your will, take this cup away from Me; nevertheless not My will, but Yours, be done."** *Then an angel appeared to Him from heaven, strengthening Him. And being in agony, He prayed more earnestly.* **Then His sweat became like great drops of blood falling down to the ground."**

Luke 22:39-44

There are two things in this text that we *must* be aware of. Jesus is praying and interceding to the Father, asking Him to take "this cup" away from Him; yet He says that He would rather be in His Father's will—not His own. This turmoil caused Him to sweat "great drops of blood." Our Lord was fighting with His flesh, mind, and emotions—to the point where Dr. Luke tells us He was sweating drops of real blood.

The first blood Jesus poured out for us was not on the cross, but in the fight He had with Himself—and won—in the garden of Gethsemane!

It is scientifically proven that under the most extreme conditions, like being in the front lines of war, soldiers and others have experienced small blood vessels bursting because of the stress causing blood drops to appear on their foreheads.

What Cup?

Luke also mentions a cup, "this cup," to be taken away from Him by God. God does not answer that prayer, but leaves it up to His Son to decide. The cup is the coming blood covenant to be made through His sacrifice on the cross—taking all our sicknesses, sins, and curses upon Himself!

He knew He would be carrying *all* our sins, curses and sicknesses. An extremely terrible death, not just a "normal" crucifixion that was evil enough! Crucifixion was a slow death, totally and shamefully exposed to the public, who would watch His sufferings until He took His last breath.

Remember the cup of wine sealing the Hebrew blood covenant? Every time we find the word "cup" in the Bible, it is covenant talk. It has something to do with a covenant!

Matthew was previously a tax collector and so he focused on different things when he wrote about the same event. In Matthew 26 we see that Jesus is using "biblical imperative," repeating His plea to the Father. The strongest way He could plea with God to avoid the cross was repeating the plea three times. In biblical times they did not have imperative or exclamation marks to indicate emphasis—rather they repeated something important.

Then Jesus came with them to a place called Gethsemane, and said to the disciples, **"Sit here while I go and pray over there."** *And He took with Him Peter and the two sons of Zebedee, and He began to be sorrowful and deeply distressed.* **Then He said to them, "My soul is exceedingly sorrowful, even to death. Stay here and watch with Me."** *He went a little farther and fell on His face, and prayed, saying, "O My* **Father, if it is possible, let this cup pass from Me; nevertheless, not as I will, but as You will."**

Then He came to the disciples and found them sleeping, and said to Peter, **"What! Could you not watch with Me one hour? Watch and pray, lest you enter into temptation. The spirit indeed is willing, but the** *flesh is weak." Again, a second time, He went away and prayed, saying, "O My **Father, if this cup cannot pass away from Me unless I drink it, Your will be done."***

Matthew 26:36-42

The Promise and Prophecy

The promise and prophecy by the prophet Isaiah in the Old Testament, 700 years before Jesus was born, is recorded in Isaiah 53:4-5:

*Surely He has borne our pain and carried our sickness; yet we esteemed Him stricken, smitten by God, and afflicted. But **He was wounded** for our transgressions, **He was bruised** for our iniquities; the chastisement for our peace was upon Him, and **by His stripes we are healed."***

This prophecy is fulfilled in two Scriptures in the New Testament, each one referring to one half of Isaiah's prophecy. We find them in First Peter 2:24 and Matthew 8:17.

*Who Himself **bore** our sins in His own body on the tree, that we, having died to sins, might live for righteousness—**by whose stripes you were healed."***

1 Peter 2:24

Do you note the past tense—"were healed"? The work is done, finished for us to receive and walk it out in faith. You have been healed by Jesus' act of sacrifice on the cross.

Jesus is ministering and healing the people to fulfill the Scripture in Isaiah:

that it might be fulfilled which was spoken by
*Isaiah the prophet, saying: **"He Himself took our***
infirmities and bore our sicknesses."
Matthew 8:17

In the Roman Empire at the time our Lord was walking the earth, one of the most normal punishments was scourging the criminals, giving them between 30-40 lashes with a very special whip.

They used a whip with strings of leather to which were tied very sharp pieces of bone or stones. When they used this torture instrument, the whip literally tore out bits and pieces of flesh from the person's back until bones in their back were exposed. The "stripes" referred to are from the scourging of Jesus, until His back was an open wound and bleeding profusely.

The person being scourged lost a lot of blood during the ordeal, and it was common for the person to enter into what the doctors call physical "shock." The person became terribly thirsty and very weak, not only from the horrible suffering, but also from the loss of blood.

Remember that the Romans commanded our Lord Jesus to carry His own cross after being scourged? A cross of solid Acacia wood normally weighed about 135 kilograms (298 pounds)! The custom was to make the criminal carry the crossbeam only, but that alone weighed about 45 kilograms (99 pounds)! The person already being scourged and weak from blood loss would struggle to even carry a modern handbag, much less a heavy crossbeam.

Scripture tells us that the Roman soldiers commanded another man to help carry the cross of our Lord, as He himself was unable (see Matthew 27:32).

How can we even begin to thank our Lord and Savior for what He did for us in the garden of Gethsemane by choosing to accept God's plan, for choosing to endure the pain and scourging, for carrying the cross (the tree—us) to Golgotha, for choosing to be nailed to the cross (the tree—us) so we can freely accept His gift of salvation and ultimately live with Him in heaven for eternity?

We can begin by living a life of loving obedience and accepting God's will rather than our will. And we can understand His sacrifice more by examining the crucifixion of the Son of God, our Redeemer.

The Success Contract

Chapter Eight

The Crucifixion

Because Jesus was obedient to His Father's plan of redemption for His created children, His crucifixion is the ultimate blood sacrifice. His is the only pure, clean, sinless blood that once and forever totally erases humankind's past, current, and future failings and sufferings—the final blood sacrifice.

There are different kinds of crucifixion in different parts of the world starting 519 B.C. This first historical record of a crucifixion was Darius, King of Persia who crucified 3,000 political opponents in Babylon.[1] But the similarity between them all is that the hideous execution was designed as a public spectacle to deter criminal activity among the people. It was a shameful, cruel, inhumane, and extremely painful form of death. Fortunately, in A.D. 337, Roman Emperor Constantine the Great abolished crucifixion as punishment; it was too cruel.[2]

The Romans used different kinds of crosses, with or without a crossbeam. However, archeology has shown that the crosses used in the time and place of our Lord's crucifixion were T-shaped, with a crossbeam. The cross was normally made of Acacia wood (see Chapter 6, The Tree section, for more details).

The Crucifixion Process

When Jesus and the soldiers arrived at the place of the execution, from my research and understanding of the Bible, I can imagine the following took place:

The cross of Acacia wood was placed flat on the ground and Jesus was laid on top of it with His bloody, tortured back against the long center rail and His arms stretched straight out on top of the crossbeam. They stretched Him as much as possible.

Next they nailed Jesus' wrists and feet to the cross using 13-18 centimeter (5-7 inch) nails. The nails were normally hammered through the person's wrists rather than the hands. The hands would not support the person's weight, unless the arms were also tied with ropes and when the cross was lifted upright, the nails would slice through the hands. The feet were put one on top of the other, and a large nail was hammered through both. Sometimes they would also nail the feet to each side of the cross; but in the case of Jesus, they nailed them to each other on top of a support made of the same kind of wood.

Both the nails through the hands and the nail through the feet bruised His central nerve that runs through the whole body, causing excruciating pain to shoot continuously through His body. It is the same pain felt when we hit a certain point of our elbow, the central nerve—multiplied 1,000 times!

The cross with Jesus nailed to it was abruptly hoisted upright and dropped into a hole in the ground. He would try to support himself, using His already bruised feet to push Himself upward. Why? To be able to breathe! When the cross was standing upright, the two nails in His wrists were the only points holding up His body. After He could no longer push up with His feet, Jesus slowly suffocated, His collarbone dislocated because of the weight.

This horrible process of dying could last for hours or even days, before the person finally died from suffocation. The Bible says that no bones in Jesus' body would be broken (see John 19:36). This is significant because the soldiers normally broke the legs of the person so the process would go faster, and the suffering was shortened. When the legs were broken, the person could no longer push upward and so died within minutes.

Our Lord went through this whole terrible process for us!

Our Lord went through this whole terrible process for us, first being scourged so His back was an open wound with bones visible and blood dripping. After being nailed to the cross, He went through a certain time, as the prophet Isaiah says, of being twisted and crushed, carrying all of our sins, pains, and curses in His own body, emotions, mind, and Spirit (see Isaiah 53:4-5).

For the first time in Jesus' life, He was disconnected and left by His Father God (see Isaiah 53:6). He was identified 100 percent with humankind, who had been disconnected from God since sinning in the Garden of Eden (see Isaiah 53:11).

I understand this to be the most horrible part for Jesus, cold and alone, left by His always-present, loving Father. This is the only time in this process we hear Jesus shouting loudly, "Father, Father, why have You forsaken Me?" (See Matthew 27:45.)

A little while later, Jesus decides to give up His Spirit and die.

Jesus Christ never had His legs broken. To fulfill Scripture, but also because He was demonstrating to the world that He chose to die by His own will at His own timing. The crucifixion of our Lord Jesus ends with Him shouting loudly, *IT IS FINISHED!*" (See John 19:30.)

Was it really possible? The soldiers looking at Him were terrified and said, *"Truly this was the Son of God!"* (See Matthew 27:54.) Why did they say that? Because they had executed many hundred criminals and they knew that it was impossible to shout with a loud voice when a person was dying of suffocation! No one can possibly scream out loud when his voice is gone and his tongue is trapped in his throat.

A Special Sign

At exactly the same moment Jesus decided to give up His Spirit, the curtain in the Temple was torn into two parts.

Now this was *not* a normal little curtain in a small kitchen window. This thing was 6 meters (about 20 feet) tall and 10 centimeters (about 4 inches) thick, all woven in one single piece!

Not even four strong oxen pulling it from opposite sides could tear it in two. Yet at the same moment Jesus shouted, "It is finished" and died, this monster curtain was torn in two all by itself—by God! (See Matthew 27:51.)

Reconciliation with God and the "bridge" back to unity with Father God was a reality. The curtain in the Temple was forever opened; and what hindered you and me from going directly to throne of the Father was taken away forever.

From that moment on, salvation and the prayer of faith and commitment was and continues to be the way into the Holy of Holies. The "Door" has a name—Jesus Christ—and no one comes to Father God unless the person passes through Jesus (see John 10:9; 14:6).

Not only was Jesus nailed to the cross, but also every sin we ever committed, are committing, and will ever commit. He brought hope to our hearts—hope and peace deep down within that we can't possibly understand. He brings emotional healing and restoration in ways that defy logical reasoning and speaks solely to our spiritual inner self. Through World Impact Ministries, we help people who are hurting realize what Jesus did for them through the crucifixion.

Before Jesus died on the cross, all people were separated from God, manifested in guilt, fear, shame, and spiritual death. Their true identity was destroyed, they were robbed of their dignity, and their authority was corrupted—the consequences of disobedience by the first humans in the Garden of Eden. The evil that slithered into their lives affected and influenced all creation ... until the very moment that Jesus shed His blood life for the redemption of all.

Because of the crucifixion, because Jesus gave His life upon the cross to set us free, we can be free indeed! Hallelujah!

Endnotes

1. http://religion.lilithezine.com/History-of-Crucifixion.html; accessed 23 October 2014.

2. http://christianity.about.com/od/goodfriday/a/crucifixionhist. htm; accessed 6 October 2014.

Chapter Nine

Blood Covenant Examples in the Bible

As previously mentioned, there are blood covenants written about in the Word of God, in both the Old Testament and the New Testament.

Between Two People
David and Jonathan

We have read this Scripture before, but let us go back to First Samuel 18:1-5 again to determine what David and Jonathan were doing.

> *Now when he had finished speaking to Saul, the soul of Jonathan was knit to the soul of David, and Jonathan loved him as his own soul. Saul took him that day, and would not let him go home to his father's house anymore.* **Then Jonathan and David made a**

covenant, because he loved him as his own soul.
And Jonathan took off the robe *that was on him
and gave it to David, with his armor, even to his
sword and his bow* **and his belt.** *So David went
out wherever Saul sent him, and behaved wisely.
And Saul set him over the men of war, and he was
accepted in the sight of all the people and also in the
sight of Saul's servants.*

1 Samuel 18:1-5

Can you see what kind of covenant David and Jonathan
were making? Correct, they were cutting a blood covenant.
Even if the Bible only shares a few of the things they did, it
is enough to understand what they were doing. They were
exchanging *mantles* (robes): "All that they were and all that
they had," and *belts* (protection until death).

Jonathan and David exchanged all they were and all they
had with each other. That included their status in life. They
became one and friends for the rest of their lives. Whoever
died first left all to the other. Now, remember that Jonathan
was the son of King Saul, the prince and legal heir to the
kingdom of Israel. So after becoming blood covenant
friends, they shared everything; and as David was one
with Jonathan, *he was the legal heir to the throne if Jonathan
died.* As you probably know, Jonathan did die, and that left
David as the legal heir to the throne!

We know that God anointed David king, spiritually, as a
very young man, but now we see that the people of Israel

knew exactly what the blood covenant meant between Prince Jonathan and David. When the time came, they accepted David as the legally chosen king.

Typical for our God is that He does things thoroughly. Not only was David anointed spiritually by the prophet, he was now cutting a blood covenant with the heir to the throne Jonathan, becoming "coheir" to the throne of Israel.

Elijah and Elisha

We find in First Kings 19:16-21:

"Also you shall anoint Jehu the son of Nimshi as king over Israel. And Elisha the son of Shaphat of Abel Meholah you shall anoint as prophet in your place. It shall be that whoever escapes the sword of Hazael, Jehu will kill; and whoever escapes the sword of Jehu, Elisha will kill. Yet I have reserved seven thousand in Israel, all whose knees have not bowed to Baal, and every mouth that has not kissed him."

So he departed from there, and found Elisha the son of Shaphat, who was plowing with twelve yoke of oxen before him, and he was with the twelfth. Then Elijah passed by him and threw his mantle on him. *And he left the oxen and ran after Elijah, and said, "Please let me kiss my father and my mother, and then I will follow you." And he said to him,*

"Go back again, for what have I done to you?" **So Elisha turned back from him, and took a yoke of oxen and slaughtered them and boiled their flesh, using the oxen's equipment, and gave it to the people, and they ate.** *Then he arose and followed Elijah, and became his servant.*

In this example we see clearly two things related to a blood covenant. Elijah threw his *mantle* on Elisha, who instantly stopped plowing and followed Elijah as his servant. Elisha immediately knew what this meant, and it provoked several actions from him.

First and foremost they lived in a time when blood covenants were common knowledge. The young man Elisha was a wealthy heir, the son of a rich father. He was plowing with twelve yokes of oxen, not one. Elijah was a well-known prophet and the voice of God in the same time.

When the prophet Elijah threw his mantle over him as he passed by, he knew that this was a covenant and *that all that the prophet Elijah had and all he was were given to him, Elisha, from that moment on.*

The second thing showing the blood covenant is Elisha breaking the yoke into pieces and *killing an ox* (pure animal), making a burnt sacrifice and using the yoke of wood to burn the flesh.

Elisha asked for permission to say goodbye to his parents, and from that moment he started following his new blood covenant partner and mentor, Elijah, as his servant. Later in his life, when Elijah was taken to heaven, Elisha received the mantle again, falling on him from above; and not only did he get exactly the same anointing as Elijah, he received it double strong.

Remember that the mantle represents everything a person is and has, and Elisha had asked for a double portion.

God and Humankind

We also find covenants and blood covenants between *God and humankind*. After Adam sinned, God decided to make a protection covenant with His first man, Adam.

In Genesis 3:21 we find proof of a blood covenant taking place: *"Also for Adam and his wife the Lord God made tunics of skin, and clothed them."* God killed, shed the blood of an animal, to make Adam and Eve tunics of animal skin. Tunics or mantels signify God's intent: "All I am and all I have is yours for protection." The problem was it had to be repeated every year to be valid. This took place in the Old Testament, about 4,000 years before God sent His Son Jesus.

We also know there were many consequences humankind had to suffer because Adam and Eve broke the first covenant with God when *they agreed* to eat the fruit of the tree of the knowledge of good and evil (see Genesis 2:16-17; 3:6).

The world we see around us today is the consequence of humankind's sin. What would we have done without the mercy and sacrifice that made us a New Blood Covenant as Father God offered up His own Son to die! It is so very important to share this Good News with the broken and destroyed world in which we live.

In the Bible we see God make blood covenants with Noah, Abraham, Isaac, Jacob (later Israel), Moses, and David. Many times the Bible does not mention any specific details about the blood covenant, but it is easy to discern by the promises and the fruits of the different covenants.

God and Job and Job's Friends

One of the blood covenants I find very interesting in the Word of God is in the oldest book of the Bible, the book of Job.

You can read the whole story for yourself; it is all about Job, a real servant of God of whom God is very proud because he is so righteous in all that he does.

But Job has a big fear. His children are not very righteous and not well-behaved, so Job goes around in constant fear of something happening to them.

The devil is accusing Job before God all the time, telling God it is easy for Job to be a good man, because God is spoiling him with wealth and everything else. The devil is given the right to test Job, and he starts by killing his children, but Job continues to worship God. The devil launches a lot of attacks and robs Job of everything, only to find Job is still worshipping God. Finally the devil says to God, "Job has a covenant of protection with You. How can I test if he will still worship You without that protection as long as he is protected?" (see Job 1:9-11; 2:4-5).

God allows the devil to test Job as he likes, but he is not permitted to take his life. Job still has a covenant of protection of his life with God. In the process of the testing Job loses everything he has, his children and his wealth. He also gets very sick and is sitting in self-pity, but he never blames God. Everyone has left him including his family and relatives. His wife stays and complains.

Then a blood covenant suddenly kicks into action and suddenly we see three *friends* appear (see Job 2:11). Everybody else had left Job; why would these three friends come just now? They had to! They obviously had a blood covenant with Job from earlier when he was a successful and rich man and they were obligated to help and support Job. Calling them friends shows us that they were blood covenant friends of Job. These were the only people called friends during this time of the patriarchs.

The friends give the most terrible advice to Job, but they stick with him out of obligation. Job finally is convinced by his friends to complain to God for his condition. God rebukes him and he repents:

Moreover the Lord answered Job, and said: "Shall the one who contends with the Almighty correct Him? He who rebukes God let him answer it." Then Job answered the Lord and said: "Behold, I am vile; what shall I answer You? I lay my hand over my mouth. Once I have spoken, but I will not answer; yes, twice, but I will proceed no further."

Job 40:1-5

Basically what Job is saying is, "I will shut up. You are God and know best!" Then something very important happens: God asks Job to pray for his friends and *He will make a new covenant with him.* See if you can recognize what is happening in these next few verses:

*And **the Lord restored Job's losses when he prayed for his friends.** Indeed the Lord gave Job twice as much as he had before. Then all **his brothers, all his sisters, and all those who had been his acquaintances before, came to him and ate food with him in his house;** and they consoled him and comforted him for all the adversity that the Lord had brought upon him. **Each one gave him a piece of silver and each a ring of gold.** Now the Lord blessed the latter days of Job more than his beginning…*

Job 42:10-13

Can you see the blood covenant? People came back to Job and not only did they make a sacrifice of clean animals but the family was reconciled and everyone gave Job a piece of silver and rings of gold. Pretty hidden is it not? A pure blood covenant with exchanging of gifts.

I believe there are many treasures hidden in the Word of God. The more we study the Hebrew blood covenant the more the Word opens up to us. It is really life changing.

Jesus and You and Me

Almost every time we see the word "cup" in the Bible it is covenant talk. Every time we see the word "friend," it is the same. Let me end this section of examples with our Lord Jesus when He speaks covenant in John 17. Knowing He was going to the cross to cut a new and better eternal blood covenant, unbreakable and enabling us to receive Him as our Lord and forever be reconciled to the Father, Jesus prays:

> *I do not pray for these alone, but also for those who will believe in Me through their word [that would be us!];* ***that they all may be one, as You, Father, are in Me, and I in You; that they also may be one in Us,*** *that the world may believe that You sent Me. And the glory, which You gave Me I have given them, that they may be one just as We are one:* ***I in them, and You in Me; that they may be made perfect in one,*** *and that the world*

*may know that You have sent Me, and **have loved***
them as You have loved Me.
John 17:20-23

Jesus is talking blood covenant talk: I in You, You in Me; We in them and they in Us! We are no longer independent people, as Jesus is one with the Father, we now are one with Him, and "in Him" with the Father.

We are also one with each other as Christian brothers and sisters!

That is why Jesus hates division in His body, the church. Division means we have not understood that we are one and friends forever according to the blood covenant made by our Lord. A blood covenant we have entered into through salvation in Him.

Chapter Ten

The Old and New Blood Covenants

B lood covenants are found in the Bible in both the Old Testament (Covenant) and the New Testament (Covenant). Examples of blood covenants in the Old Covenant include the circumcision of the flesh. Before Jesus came to redeem humankind, people's nature was sinful, and every year they needed to sacrifice clean, pure animals to cover their sins.

The Old Covenant

The covenant initiated by God with Moses at Mount Sinai was ratified through blood sacrifices:

> *Now therefore, if you will indeed obey My voice and*
> ***keep My covenant***, *then you shall be a special treasure*
> *to Me above all people; for all the earth is Mine."*
> **Exodus 19:5**

*And Moses took half the blood and put it in basins, and half the blood he sprinkled on the altar. Then he took the **Book of the Covenant** and read in the hearing of the people. And they said, "All that the Lord has said we will do, and be obedient." And Moses **took the blood, sprinkled it on the people**, and said, "This is the **blood of the covenant which the Lord has made with you** according to all these words."*

Exodus 24:6-8

*But into the second part the high priest went alone **once a year, not without blood**, which he offered for himself and for the people's sins committed in ignorance."*

Hebrews 9:7

This blood covenant did not annul the Abrahamic covenant:

*Now to Abraham and his Seed were the promises made. He does not say, "And to seeds," as of many, but as of one, "And to your Seed," who is Christ. And this I say, that **the law**, which was four hundred and thirty years later, **cannot annul the covenant that was confirmed before by God in Christ**, that it should make the promise of no effect. For if the inheritance is of the law, it is no longer of promise; but God gave it to Abraham by promise.*

Galatians 3:16-18

The law was to point us to Christ:

*Therefore the **law was our tutor to bring us to Christ**, that we might be justified by faith. But after faith has come, we are no longer under a tutor.*

Galatians 3:24-25

The law consists in the outward Tabernacle:

Now when these things had been thus prepared, the priests always went into the first part of the tabernacle, performing the services.

Hebrews 9:6

The covenant was sealed through circumcision:

This is My covenant which you shall keep, between Me and you and your descendants after you: Every male child among you shall be circumcised; and you shall be circumcised in the flesh of your foreskins, and it shall be a sign of the covenant between Me and you.

Genesis 17:10-11

The New Covenant

Our faith in the blood of Jesus and the circumcision of the Spirit gives us the new birth and total annulation of sin. The New Covenant—the new birth in Christ—was promised by

God way back in the Garden of Eden and also proclaimed to Abraham.

> *And I will put enmity between you and the woman,*
> *and between your seed and her Seed; He shall bruise*
> *your head, and you shall bruise His heel."*
>
> **Genesis 3:15**

> *I will bless those who bless you, and I will curse him who curses*
> *you; and in you all the families of the earth shall be blessed.*
>
> **Genesis 12:3**

The New Covenant and new birth was dated in Daniel's prophecy:

> *Seventy weeks are determined for your people and for*
> *your holy city, to finish the transgression, to make*
> *an end of sins, to make reconciliation for iniquity, to*
> *bring in everlasting righteousness, to seal up vision*
> *and prophecy, and to anoint the Most Holy. Know*
> *therefore and understand, that from the going forth*
> *of the command to restore and build Jerusalem until*
> *Messiah the Prince, there shall be seven weeks and*
> *sixty-two weeks; the street shall be built again, and*
> *the wall, even in troublesome times. And after the*
> *sixty-two weeks Messiah shall be cut off, but not*
> *for Himself; and the people of the prince who is to*
> *come shall destroy the city and the sanctuary. The*

end of it shall be with a flood, and till the end of the war desolations are determined. Then he shall confirm a covenant with many for one week; but in the middle of the week He shall bring an end to sacrifice and offering. And on the wing of abominations shall be one who makes desolate, even until the consummation, which is determined, is poured out on the desolate.

Daniel 9:24-27

The ultimate blood covenant was fulfilled in Christ Jesus as was told in the prophecy of Zacharias spoken over John the Baptist:

*Blessed is the Lord God of Israel, for He has visited and redeemed His people, and has raised up a horn of salvation for us in the house of His servant David, as He spoke by the mouth of His holy prophets, who have been since the world began, that we should be saved from our enemies and from the hand of all who hate us, to perform the mercy promised to our fathers and to **remember His holy covenant**, the oath which He swore to our father Abraham: to grant us that we, being delivered from the hand of our enemies, might serve Him without fear, in holiness and righteousness before Him all the days of our life. And you, child, will be called the prophet of the Highest; for you will go before the face of the Lord to prepare His ways, **to give knowledge of salvation*** *to His people by the remission of their sins, through the tender mercy of our God, with which the Dayspring from on high has visited us; to give light to those who sit in darkness and the shadow of death, to guide our feet into the way of peace.*

Luke 1:68-79

The New Covenant was ratified in the blood of Jesus:

*Not with the blood of goats and calves, but **with His own blood** He entered the Most Holy Place once for all, having obtained eternal redemption.*

Hebrews 9:12

The New Covenant is remembered in the Lord's Supper and is called eternal, everlasting:

*In the same manner He also took the cup after supper, saying, "This cup is **the new covenant in My blood.** This do, as often as you drink it, in remembrance of Me.*

1 Corinthians 11:25

*Now may the God of peace who brought up our Lord Jesus from the dead, that great Shepherd of the sheep, **through the blood of the everlasting covenant.***

Hebrews 13:20

Chapter Eleven

Hindrances to Living Out God's Blessings

I'm sure you have by now a good idea of how strong and powerful you are as a child of God and co-heir with Christ in the Kingdom. The goal of this book is to show you more clearly who you are in Christ through the blood covenant of salvation. I'm blessed to know you are in the process of maturing and becoming more like our Lord, Leader, and Covenant Friend Jesus.

So why isn't every child of God walking and living in this authority and power?

The following are four important hindrances that keep us from walking in the power and authority of the Kingdom of God while we are living here on earth. Some you might know—others might be totally new revelations. I pray you will seriously consider and pray about each one.

1. **Living in a Relationship Outside of Marriage**

2. **Sexual Abuse or Rape**

3. **Generational Curses**

4. **Unforgiveness and Criticism**

We will review each of these four areas in depth.

Living in a Relationship Outside of Marriage

The covenant of marriage is a true blood covenant and has many spiritual implications. The man and woman in a blood covenant exchange everything, all that they are and all that they have, good and bad.

If you are living in an intimate relationship outside of marriage or frequently changing partners, something very normal today, you will have several blood covenants. This means that all the bad and all the good that every person had while being intimate with you, you now have.

I have been ministering emotional healing and restoration to women and men for more than 20 years, and the following truth is shared from my real-life experience: as a minister I can pray for you, but *blood covenants are personal. Where there is a blood covenant, you yourself have to pray and renounce it to stop and break its hold over you.*

Hindrances to Living Out God's Blessing

The following is my suggestion on how you can break unhealthy blood covenants. Being a child of God, you need to *repent and renounce every blood covenant you ever made by being in an intimate relationship with another person, outside of marriage.*

If you have been married several times, *the spouses you are not living with now need to be renounced and cut from your life.* You need to name every person, or if you do not remember the name, mention the person by the situation. You and God know who you mean.

Your prayer may be something like this:

Father, in the name of Jesus, please forgive me for having violated Your blood covenant and sinned. I renounce everything that (mention the name) has given to me, and I take back all that I have given to (name). I cut every physical tie, every emotional tie, every spiritual and mental tie with (name), and I proclaim myself free from (name)!

Repeat this prayer, using each person's name, for every intimate relationship you have ever had.

Forming a blood covenant relationship is so much more serious than most understand in this day and age of casual, intimate liaisons. After you pray this prayer to God, you should note a difference in your peace of mind, soul, and spirit.

Sexual Abuse or Rape

Sadly, worldwide there are many children who have been abused sexually and raped. There are also many women who never reported the abuse or rape and don't even talk about it because of the shame and pain associated with the experience.

The violator caused a blood covenant to take place without the other person's consent, which leaves deep wounds within the victim.

How many times have you heard women say, "I seem to always attract the wrong kind of man, over and over again. Men who abuse me, who are violent, who drink, etc."

When a person is abused or sexually violated, all the perverse demons and junk the violator carries are passed on, even as a child! These evil powers have the "right" to live within the person until there is something done about it personally.

There is definitely something to be done! Victims can proclaim themselves free from the abuser by cutting all ties! If you have been a victim of abuse—sexual, mental, physical, emotional—you can cut yourself free today, right now, by praying the prayer above. God is faithful to heal your wounds.

You, now being aware of the implications of a blood covenant, can explain to other people: "You need to pray to renounce the blood covenant made and proclaim yourself free from the person who abused you." The blood covenant violation follows the person and his or her family for generations as curses. I have seen great liberations take place by praying the prayer. All the horrible "flashbacks" and "mental pictures" haunting a person for years suddenly disappear. *God sets people free from covenants through the blood covenant in Jesus Christ and the name of Jesus, which is stronger than any other name and covenant!*

Feel free to contact my ministry for more information on this subject, using our contact information at the end of this book. We minister in these areas frequently and can help you heal.

Generational Curses

Another hindrance that may be keeping you from walking in the abundant life of the new blood covenant in Christ is generational curses.

If you know there have been children born out of wedlock in your family, through adultery or fornication, it is very likely that something has been passed down through the generations to you and your children.

Someone before you has sinned and broken the blood covenant, and as a result curses are affecting them *and their family.*

A generational curse may manifest as depression, addiction, or sickness. For example, your mother had cancer and your grandmother had cancer. Maybe you are depressed, your aunt is depressed, and your grandfather suffered from depression.

Many medical doctors nowadays talk about genetically inherited sickness, but we know that the blood covenant in Jesus Christ can totally break any curse of sickness and stop it forever from going down your family lines.

The blood covenant in Jesus Christ can totally break any curse or sickness and stop it forever from going down your family lines.

To ensure no generational curse exists, you can pray a prayer to break it. You can spiritually put yourself in the "gap" for your ancestors. Because they are your family members, you have the authority to pray on behalf of those who have passed away (not people still alive, they have to repent themselves).

Suggested prayer to break generational curses:

Father God, in the name of Jesus, I put myself in the gap for my ancestors. I ask You for forgiveness for any sin committed by them or through them. I renounce any blood covenant through fornication or adultery on their behalf, and cancel any curse that has been

created as a result of such a blood covenant that has
come on my family and me. I proclaim myself free!

Any child born out of wedlock, fruits of an adulterous relationship (intimate relationship with a person while married to someone else) or fornication (intimate relationship *without being married* to the person), causes a curse for ten generations.

> **One of illegitimate birth** *shall not enter the assembly*
> *of the Lord;* ***even to the tenth generation*** *none of his*
> *descendants shall enter the assembly of the Lord.*
> **Deuteronomy 23:2**

Because of the new blood covenant with Jesus that is powerful and able to save, we can pray and turn this around for ourselves and for our children after us. We always pray to the Father in the name of Jesus, because that is what the Lord has instructed us to do, so we may have what we ask and pray.

The Lord Jesus tells us in John 15:16:

> *You did not choose Me, but I chose you and appointed*
> *you that you should go and bear fruit, and that your*
> *fruit should remain,* ***that whatever you ask the***
> ***Father in My name He may give you.***

Other hindrances may be holding you back from living in abundance in your new blood covenant in Christ where there is protection, health, peace, joy, and more than enough resources. You will surely recognize some of these things, *but are you willing to pray about them and change your behavior, lifestyle, habits, etc.?*

Or do you just say and think, "Jesus loves me just as I am"? I am sure you are right, but that does not mean you are living in Him and His provisions, as you could do after understanding and taking seriously the implications of a blood covenant.

We read in Galatians 5 about all the works of the flesh and the bad fruits they cause. I would like to emphasize the end of that chapter to see where evil leads us if there is no repentance and change in our lives:

*Now the works of the flesh are evident, which are: adultery, fornication, uncleanness, lewdness, idolatry, sorcery, hatred, contentions, jealousies, outbursts of wrath, selfish ambitions, dissensions, heresies, envy, murders, drunkenness, revelries, and the like; of which I tell you beforehand, just as I also told you in time past, **that those who practice such things will not inherit the kingdom of God.***
Galatians 5:19-21

It seems quite clear to me where we are going if we don't repent and change our way of living.

Unforgiveness and Criticism
Two serious hindrances to living in
success and abundance!

Let us first talk about unforgiveness. The Word of God is very clear on this:

But if you do not forgive men their trespasses, neither will your Father forgive your trespasses.
Matthew 6:15

But if you do not forgive, neither will your Father in heaven forgive your trespasses.
Mark 11:26

I do *not* have the luxury of not forgiving another person, even if what that person did was totally wrong and unjust.

We need to let God judge the person, and I really believe He is much more capable of doing that than we are. God will judge the person *if you let go and forgive*. God takes notice when someone harms one of His anointed children (you and me). Unforgiveness may eventually cause you to lose your right to enter the Kingdom of heaven. Please don't allow that to happen.

You might be in a situation where you can forgive people around you, but you cannot forgive yourself for something you did.

The Success Contract

One of the places we often find this while ministering emotional healing is in women who have had abortions. Even if it was a miscarriage, a lot of women feel guilty.

If you have had a provoked abortion or a miscarriage, please read this part carefully.

First, I want you to know that your baby is with Jesus, he or she was not lost. Secondly, you need to forgive yourself and release your baby. We have had so many wonderful deliverances of women with these simple steps.

1. If the abortion was provoked, ask God to forgive you for killing your baby. Let me remind you of a verse from the Bible: 1 John 1:9 says, *"If we confess our sins, He is faithful and just to forgive us our sins and to cleanse us from all unrighteousness."* It says "all" – that includes everything!

2. Ask God if your baby was a boy or a girl. He will tell you, or give you a feeling one way or the other – He will let you know.

3. Now that you know the sex of your baby: Name your child.

4. Pray and release the baby into the arms of God

   Father, in the name of Jesus, I release (baby's name) into your arms. I thank you that you care for him/ her for me until the day I get to heaven.

5. Break a spirit of death over your womb. If the abortion was provoked, break also a spirit of murder.

Father, in the name of Jesus I break a spirit of death (and a spirit of murder) over my womb. I thank you for filling my womb up with your life.

What about criticism—criticizing others? In my experience, this is one of the most evil sins and hardest habits to break, and it is found rampant everywhere today—including in the Body of Christ, the Church.

Criticism is really "murdering" with words (and thoughts), due to pride, hate, jealousy, or insecurity. Criticism is being proud, putting yourself over other people and judging them! The Bible says judge not or you will be judged (see Matthew 7:1). God says *He* will judge, and He is really the only One who can, as He sees all the hearts and all the intentions (see Psalm 9:8). He is the only One with access to the "whole package," so to speak.

Where there is unforgiveness, there will normally be criticism and hate too. We are children of God and siblings in the Kingdom, we need to stop criticizing and do what the Second Commandment says: Love your neighbor (and others) like yourself. When we show love for each other, society will recognize us as God's children. What a big responsibility

Where unforgiveness if found, criticism and hate follow.

God has put on us Christians, to be examples of love and caring so the world can "see" God and be saved!

I believe we can and will love each other when we understand what we really have in and through the new blood covenant in Christ Jesus. I also believe that we know when we are living in any kind of sin, because the conviction of the Holy Spirit will be very strong in our lives. This is always true unless we decide to continue in sin over a long period of time. Then we become immune to the still, small voice of God—we choose not to hear Him.

Hurry up and repent, ask for forgiveness and change your life!

A good Scripture for daily use in your prayer time to make sure you keep living a life that glorifies God is 1 John 1:9:

"If we confess our sins, He is faithful and just to forgive us our sins and to cleanse us from all unrighteousness."

You and I really do not want to "crucify our Lord" over and over again by sinning and breaking His blood covenant. That hurts our beloved Lord and Savior. Let us get hold of everything we possibly can with the power and authority available to us by walking out our salvation, maturing and repenting from anything that may hinder us.

Hindrances to Living Out God's Blessing

The overall vision of God for humanity, His goal and passion, we find in Habakkuk 2:14:

"For the earth will be filled with the knowledge of the glory of the Lord, as the waters cover the sea."

God wants to see the whole earth saved and reconciled with Him. If we each do our part, we are one step closer to seeing God's vision fulfilled.

The Success Contract

Chapter Twelve

Marketplace Application

What Is the Marketplace?

The "marketplace" is the term used for where we work in society. If you are not employed in a local church, you are working in the marketplace.

Your life every day at work is a very important part of living your life in the blood covenant with Christ. Whether you own a business or you are employed by someone, you still need to fulfill certain criteria of the blood covenant with God. You need to make Jesus Christ the Lord over both your personal life and your work.

If you run your own business, is it your business or His? If you are employed, do you just work to get your paycheck, or do you work for your boss as onto God?

The blood covenant between you and Jesus demands integrity and honesty in all parts of your life and work.

Our Purpose

As Christians it is our purpose to bring the Kingdom of God and Christ to our businesses, workplaces, professions, universities, schools, city halls, governments, and politicians.

We all need to serve God in the local church, but a lot of people have their principal calling in the marketplace. You need to understand clearly that your calling to the marketplace *is a valid ministry from God* if you are not called into full-time ministry in the church.

All ministries operating in the church are also operating in the marketplace, including the fivefold ministries and all kinds of helps ministries. There are Christians who have an *anointing* for the fivefold ministry (apostle, prophet, teacher, evangelist, and pastor), but their *calling* is to the marketplace, not the church. They attend and serve in their church, but their *primary calling* is to the marketplace

A typical apostolic fivefold ministry calling to the marketplace is a business leader who is planting several businesses, initiating new innovations, and taking numerous calculated risks.

The same with the fivefold pastoral calling, being typically called to professions of caring and serving people such as medical doctors, nurses, even leaders who help businesses survive and function. I'm sure you can think of examples of the fivefold calling of teachers, prophets, and evangelists as well.

There are people working in helps ministries in the marketplace such as musicians, singers, writers, counselors, and others.

The Goal of a Marketplace Calling

Our key calling to the marketplace is to be the tool God uses *to introduce Christ to the marketplace and the people in the marketplace to Christ.*

The following are examples from the Bible:

God uses the symbol of a donkey to explain business and work: *"Binding his **donkey to the vine**, and his donkey's colt to the choice vine, he washed his garments in wine, and his clothes in the blood of grapes* (Genesis 49:11). This is the prophetic word Jacob spoke over his son, Judah.

In the Old Testament, the donkey was used as an animal to carry loads, burdens to the market. It was the boxcar or van of that time. In Genesis 49:11, God is saying "Stay close and bind your work or business to Me, to the Vine, so that it may be protected by My blood, the wine!"

In the Old Blood Covenant of protection, through the Law, people needed to be bound to God by sacrifices. In the New Testament, the donkey (your work or business) is released when you bring it with you to the Lord Jesus. It is the New Blood Covenant in Christ that set free you and all you are and have—as long as you give it all to Him, Jesus. As I said, you need to ask yourself: *"Is it your business or His?"*

In Matthew 21:2-3 Jesus told His disciples:

> *... Go into the village opposite you, and immediately you will find a donkey tied, and a colt with her. Loose them and bring them to Me. And if anyone says anything to you, you shall say, "The Lord has need of them," and immediately he will send them.*

A donkey that is bound to anything other than God means your business or working life is bound in slavery, without freedom. It is an expression of the curse that came with the sin. Freedom comes as a result of obedience and fulfilling the Word of God. The donkey (your business or work) is set free when you admit that "the Lord has need of it." The King wants to manifest His lordship over your professional and personal life—for His purpose to be fulfilled.

After people convert to Christ, their donkey has to be "saved" too. Their profession, company, working life must be dedicated to the Lord—committing its mission and vision to furthering His Kingdom. Remember in a blood covenant: *All* I have is yours and all you have is mine!

Two Sides of a Covenant Business

Natural	Spiritual
Business Idea	Calling and the Vision
Product	Obedience
Market	Faith
Success	Fruits
Freedom	Stewardship
Testimony	Manifestation
Position	Kingdom Heir

---

*Therefore know that the Lord your God, He is God, the faithful God who keeps covenant and mercy **for a thousand generations with those who love Him and keep His commandments** .*

Deuteronomy 7:9

Keep Living in the Blessing!

Be sure to routinely check your spiritual situation at your work or business. Release everything into the wonderful hands of Jesus and start giving your way to total success in all areas of life.

As ambassadors of Christ in the marketplace as well as at home and in the community, Isaiah 61:1-3 is a good passage to keep in mind—actually they are three excellent Scripture verses to memorize:

> *The Spirit of the Lord God is upon Me, because the Lord has anointed Me to preach good tidings to the poor; He has sent Me to heal the brokenhearted, to proclaim liberty to the captives, and the opening of the prison to those who are bound; to proclaim the acceptable year of the Lord, and the day of vengeance of our God; to comfort all who mourn, to console those who mourn in Zion, to give them beauty for ashes, the oil of joy for mourning, the garment of praise for the spirit of heaviness; that they may be called trees of righteousness, the planting of the Lord, that He may be glorified.*

We must do our part to keep the success contract viable and profitable—the more people we preach good tidings to, the more people will be healed, set free, and filled with joy. Fulfilling our part of the contract results in our eternal reward as well as our earthly thrill of experiencing God's best at home, work, and play.

In the next chapter we will examine covenant economy and giving.

Chapter Thirteen

Kingdom Economy = Extreme Promised Abundance

To Live in Abundance is Your Choice!

The Biblical Economy or the Economy of the Kingdom is all about *giving and receiving*.

Jesus Himself talks about different kinds of seed and the fruit that grows from them. Let me give you a shortcut into an abundant financial life full of peace, good conscience, and good fruit.

The Four Covenant Ways to Give Correctly:

Firstfruits
+ Tithes
+ Offerings
+ Alms
= Abundance!

These four ways are like "fuses" that are connected to each other and are all needed to produce the maximum result! Let's go through the four very quickly and afterward we will look at each one in more detail.

- **FIRSTFRUIT—Honors God and brings blessings over your house, family, and your life forever.** The quantity is decided by the Holy Spirit, but it is normally not very much. It can be money or other things. It honors God and will line you up with someone and their anointing, calling, and gifts.

- **TITHE—Belongs to God (the local church).** It is a preparation for abundance. Tithe is 10 percent of all your income and earnings and is like a Kingdom "income tax." It belongs to God and brings protection and preparation for the blessings to follow.

- **OFFERINGS—Release a harvest of 30, 60, 100 fold of what you sow (in good soil!).** Offerings are not only money! If you sow chairs, you will harvest chairs. *If you do not name your seed, you will harvest what you sow.* You decide how much and when. If God does not ask for something specifically, it is an act of gratitude and will bring a harvest, the same thing you have sown, unless you have named what you want.

- **ALMS—Given to the poor and needy.** The Bible says alms should be given in secret to not embarrass the one who receives. Alms is lending to God, and He will repay you exactly what you give € for € ($ for $).

If you are already living by these four principles, you should be super blessed! If you are not, I suggest you re-read Chapter 11 about the hindrances to an abundant covenant life.

Now we will dive into these four covenant ways of giving and see if there is anything that you need to adjust in the way you give to God and others. Adjustments needed to be able to release financial blessings on a whole other level!

FIRSTFRUITS

- Firstfruits are all about *honoring God.*

- Firstfruits *consecrate to God the things you love.*

- Firstfruits *align you* with the anointing of the person you give them to. In other words, you get under the same anointing as the person or the ministry to which you give.

Firstfruits in relation to the New Testament Blood Covenant: *"If the **firstfruit** is holy, **the lump** is also holy; and if **the root** is holy, so are **the branches**"* [holy and consecrated] (Romans 11:16). *The firstfruit is holy* and sanctifies your whole life when you *honor* God with *the first and best part.*

Firstfruits will influence all areas of your life. God will treat it as something holy, precious, and consecrated unto Him. What you love, you sanctify to Him. Your finances are a spiritual substance that transform into a reality. Finances and honor are intertwined.

Proverbs 3:9-10 says:

*"Honor the Lord with your possessions, and with **the firstfruits of all your increase.** So your barns will be filled with plenty, and your vats will overflow with new wine."*

Ezekiel 44:30 says:

*"**The best of all firstfruits of any kind,** and every sacrifice from all your sacrifices, shall be the priest's; also you shall give to the priest the first of your ground meal, to [**cause**] a blessing to **rest** on your **house.**"*

Cause = the result of giving the firstfruits

Rest = stay permanently (forever)

House = you and the coming generations after you

To give your firstfruit is about giving the first and the best, not about giving a lot. Giving firstfruits will bring blessings over your children for generations to come—forever!

We give the firstfruits to the high priest (Old Testament) or an apostle or apostolic ministry (New Testament). Jesus is our High Priest and Apostle (see Hebrews 3:1).

The Spring Harvest

The Jews had and still have two important spring crops, barley and wheat, but in ancient Israel none of the grain could be eaten until the firstfruits of the grain had been offered. This happened after the first Sabbath of the Festival of Unleavened Bread in March/April. This coincides with the Passover (Easter). The Jews would take a basket of grain from the first harvest, which is barley, and consecrate it to God; they sacrifice it to honor God and show gratitude.[1] It was not a large quantity—a sheaf is a small hand basket.

> *And the Lord spoke to Moses, saying, "Speak to the children of Israel, and say to them: 'When you come into the land which I give to you, and reap its harvest, then you shall bring a **sheaf** of the firstfruits of your harvest to the priest." You shall eat neither bread nor parched grain nor fresh grain until the same day that you have brought an offering to your God; it shall be a statute forever throughout your generations in all your dwellings.*
> **Leviticus 23:9-10,14**

Pentecost comes 50 days later as does the second harvest, which is the wheat harvest. The Jews repeat the sacrifice of giving firstfruits of the first harvest of wheat given to the priest. The wheat harvest was always a lot larger than the barley harvest.[2]

> *Count fifty days to the day after the seventh Sabbath;*
> *then you shall offer a new grain offering to the Lord. You*
> *shall bring from your dwellings two wave loaves of two-*
> *tenths of an ephah. They shall be of fine flour; they shall be*
> *baked with leaven. They are the firstfruits to the Lord.*
>
> ### Leviticus 23:16-17

The Jews pay their tithes after the whole is harvested. As you can see clearly, the firstfruits resulted in tremendous blessings in the next harvest for the Jews.

Guess what ... the same is true for you and me today!

Go with me to Jesus Christ:

1. Jesus died during Passover, cutting the new blood covenant, and rose again the third day, the day after the Sabbath—*as the Firstfruit from Father God* and the first harvest of souls!

2. Exactly 50 days later came Pentecost.

Acts 2:2 tells us that when the Holy Spirit was poured out, God's Firstfruit, Jesus Christ, caused a harvest of thousands of souls (3,000 the first day). Unfortunately, many Christians have faithfully paid their tithes for years and yet have not really seen abundance. They are protected and blessed, but financially they are lacking. The firstfruits may be the missing link. It is like missing a fuse in the string of fuses and the electricity only works half way.

Jericho—the Firstfruit of the Promised Land

When the Jews started to conquer the Promised Land, God commanded them to take no spoils from Jericho, the first city. Those spoils belonged to God as the firstfruit. God did this to be able to bless the people of Israel with abundance in the remainder of their conquests.

> *But all the silver and gold, and vessels of bronze*
> *and iron, are consecrated to the Lord; they shall*
> *come into the treasury of the Lord.*
>
> ### *Joshua 6:19*

The story of Abraham sacrificing his son Isaac (firstfruit) is found in Genesis 22:1-19. Isaac was Abraham's first legitimate son—the son he had been waiting for all his life. God waited until Isaac was a teenager before He commanded Abraham to sacrifice him as a burnt offering. Abraham obeyed *immediately* (see Genesis 22:3), knowing that because of the blood covenant he had with God, *God* was the One who had to rescue him or revive him after being sacrificed. Abraham's obedience resulted in spiritual and material abundance for him and all generations after him, including you and me.

TITHE

The tithe is 10 percent of all your income. It belongs to God and is like a *tax* to the Kingdom of God. It gives you all the benefits of the Kingdom. We can enjoy God's protection, His "Social Security," etc.

Tithing to the Kingdom of God is like paying taxes to a secular government, which provide public services that are distributed as needed. In most countries, our taxes provide police protection, roads, schools, medical care, and so on. It is the same thing with the tithe in the Kingdom of God. The tithe puts us under the protection of God. It is preparation for much more.

If we do *not* pay the tithe, we are saved, but we live under a financial curse. God cannot give us the abundance that He wants to give us. The tithe puts you in line with the spiritual authority and the anointing of the place where you give. The anointing that is over your local church where you pay your tithe is also over you.

Maybe you say that tithing is not for today. Many people believe that giving tithe is something that was under the law. That is wrong! The tithe was initiated 430 years *before* the law was given, when Abraham gave tithe to Melchizedek. We find the story in Genesis 14.

And blessed be God Most High, Who has delivered your enemies into your hand. "And he [Abram] gave him a tithe of all.

Genesis 14:20

136

Then Jesus confirms the tithe in the New Testament:

"Woe to you, scribes and Pharisees, hypocrites! **For you pay tithe** *of mint and anise and cumin, and have neglected the weightier matters of the law: justice and mercy and faith.* **These you ought to have done** *[paying the tithe], without leaving the others undone."*

Matthew 23:23

He is telling the Pharisees that "yes, it is right to pay tithe, but don't forget about justice, mercy and faith."

Promises for the Tithe

*"**Bring all the tithes** into the storehouse that there may be food in My house; **and try me** now in this," says the Lord of hosts, "if I will not open for you the windows of heaven, and pour out for you such a blessing that there will not be room enough to receive it. And I will rebuke the devourer for your sakes, so that he will not destroy the fruit of your ground, nor shall the vine fail to bear fruit for you in the field," says the Lord of hosts.*

Malachi 3:10-11

This is the only place in the Bible where God says straight out: "Try me".

Tithe is protection against the enemy. Some friends of mine were trying this out some years back. They looked at their income, and were talking about how if they *did not* pay tithe they would have 10% more from their paychecks.

They decided to try *not* paying tithes for a couple of months. Later they told me: It was like having holes in our pockets. Our washing machine broke, one of our boys broke a tooth and we got a huge dentist bill and several other things. The protection against the enemy was not there.

They started paying tithes again very fast.

Another thing that confuse people is that they say the firstfruits and the tithe is the same thing. This is not correct, look at 2 Chronicles 31:4-5:

> *Moreover he commanded the people who dwelt in Jerusalem to contribute support for the priests and the Levites, that they might devote themselves to the Law of the Lord. As soon as the commandment was circulated, the children of Israel **brought in abundance the firstfruits** of grain and wine, oil and honey, and of all the produce of the field; and they **brought in abundantly the tithe of everything.***

Firstfruits and tithes are two different things!

One more thing about the tithe that is interesting to note:

*... Then the Lord spoke to Moses, saying, "Speak thus to the Levites, and say to them: 'When you take from the children of Israel the tithes which I have given you from them as your inheritance, **then you shall offer up a heave offering of it to the Lord, a tenth of the tithe.***

Numbers 18:21-26

The local church and the apostles pay *tithe of the tithe,* normally to those who advise them spiritually or to a missionary work.

ALMS

Alms are given to the poor and needs. Alms should be given in secret, so not to embarrass the receiver. An excellent example of giving alms to the poor is found in Luke 10:25, the parable of the Good Samaritan. Matthew 6:1-4 tells us the proper way to give alms.

But when you give to the needy, do not let your left hand know what your right hand is doing.

Matthew 6:3

Promise: God gives us exactly what we have given. Euro for euro, dollar for dollar, bread for bread; exactly the thing you have given, you will receive, unless you "name your seed" with something else. If you sow a bag of food and you need a car, name your coming harvest "car."

OFFERINGS (SEED)

Seeds, or offerings, are given in faith. Mark 12:41-44 reveals the offering of the poor widow:

> *...So He called His disciples to Himself and said to them, "Assuredly, I say to you that this poor widow has put in more than all those who have given to the treasury; for they all put in out of their abundance, but she out of her poverty put in all that she had, her whole livelihood.*

Mark 4:1-9 gives us the parable of the sower:

> *...Some fell on stony ground, where it did not have much earth; and immediately it sprang up because it had no depth of earth. But when the sun was up it was scorched, and because it had no root it withered away. And some seed fell among thorns; and the thorns grew up and choked it, and it yielded no crop. But other seed fell on good ground and yielded a crop that sprang up, increased and produced: some thirtyfold, some sixty, and some a hundred....*

And Galatians 6:7 is the original of the secular version, "What goes around comes around":

Do not be deceived, God is not mocked; for whatever a man sows, that he will also reap.

Throughout the Bible we find a principle of sowing and reaping. Promise: 30, 60, 100 fold return, depending on your faith! Always sow your seed in "good soil." Sowing in good soil means to sow into other givers. Remember to always name your seed—tell God what you want as a harvest, and He is faithful to provide.

As you see, if you expect to harvest a successful, abundant life in the Kingdom, according to the promises of the blood covenant in Christ, the outcome is highly dependent on your dealings in His biblical economy.

As you read this chapter, did you find things in your life that need to be adjusted? I believe so, my friend; correct whatever you need to correct. As you have repented and prayed and corrected all the other hindrances, do so also with your finances and your economy and start running in your new free life of abundance!

Endnotes

1. http://www.gci.org/law/festivals/harvest; accessed 23 October 2014.
2. Ibid.

The Success Contract

Chapter Fourteen

Resume

To wrap up this book, I would like to remind you of *all you have and all you are*, through this very special, eternal, and powerful blood covenant that Jesus Christ cut for us.

Father God thought you were so precious and special that He decided to take the ultimate responsibility for you as the Leader and Creator of all humanity. He decided to clean up all the messes that His creation had made.

More than 6,000 years ago man was created and eventually sinned, causing all generations after him to be contaminated by the same blood that was no longer pure. The close connection with God was broken forever. Humankind could be covered in the blood from animals as a protection from God, but the close connection with the Father God was broken.

The Success Contract

Humankind's sin went through the blood from father to son and daughter, down through the generations until today. Sin is hereditary—until there is repentance.

God selected Abraham more than 4,000 years ago. Through Abraham's obedience, God could let His own Son take humankind's place in the blood covenant. Humanity was put aside and Jesus cut the blood covenant with the Father on our behalf. Consequently, the curses spelled out in Deuteronomy 28 as part of the Abrahamic covenant, were negated by the mercy of God.

Without the sacrifice of Jesus, as sinners living under the first broken blood covenant, we would have curses showering us continually. We would be spending eternity in hell if it had not been for the tremendous grace of God to sacrifice His own Son for us—for you, for me.

Jesus Christ came to earth more than 2,000 years ago to complete the work He started with the Father 4,000 years ago on behalf of Abraham and all humanity.

Through His death on the cross and His resurrection, Jesus had the right to take our sin, curses, and sickness, as He was already made one with humankind in the earlier blood covenant with Abraham. Jesus cut an eternal blood covenant with Father God once and for all in His own blood, restoring the communion and relationship between humankind and the Father.

Resume

Anyone of the two, Jesus or Abraham/humanity, could take the death penalty on the cross for breaking the covenant with God from the beginning. Jesus did! Aren't you happy? Yes!

God the Father chose to let Jesus take that death penalty and judgment for us. All the curses of Deuteronomy 28:15-68 from the Abrahamic covenant were put on Him, plus all the sins and curses from all of humankind, sinning throughout history, past, present, and future.

The *cup* Jesus was talking about when He prayed in Gethsemane contained *all these curses and more.* All of it would be put on Him as our substitute on that cross, and He understood that. Jesus was innocent, having His Father's pure blood running through His veins, He never sinned. He was the perfect, blameless sacrifice to be offered up for sinful humankind.

Not only did He take our sins, pay our debts to God, carry our sickness, burdens, and reconcile us to the Father, Jesus also eliminated all the curses that were the result of the broken covenant with God by the first created beings, Adam and Eve.

The *New Covenant in Jesus Christ* described in the book of Hebrews chapter 10 *has no curses!* This is the first blood covenant in history that has *only blessings!* We have an incredible Lord and Savior.

Every Hebrew blood covenant had blessings and curses—blessings for keeping it and curses for breaking it. The blessings and curses from Abraham's covenant, we find in Deuteronomy chapter 28. Verses 1-15 list the blessings and verses 15-68 list the curses.

The following is an example from the curses meant for us in Deuteronomy 28 that were cancelled by the love of Christ:

Deuteronomy 28:61 says:

> *Also every sickness and every plague, which is*
> *not written in this Book of the Law, will the Lord*
> *bring upon you until you are destroyed.*

All curses are cancelled, so now we need to read it like this:

> *Every sickness and every plague, which are **NOT***
> ***written in this book of the Law [Bible],***
> ***have been cancelled by Jesus Christ, and we***
> ***are healed** of all sickness attacking us!*

Among the sicknesses not written there are AIDS, cancer, Ebola, and a lot of our "modern" sicknesses and plagues.

Dear reader, if you are a child of God, take hold of this revelation of *what is yours* and what was bought for you for such a terrible price. Check yourself, your life, and your ways. Make sure you repent and change anything that may keep you away from, or hinder you from, entering fully into the power and authority of the blood covenant you have in Christ Jesus! You have more power in your little finger than all the powers of darkness combined.

Resume

You need to believe for an abundant and successful life in Christ, full of peace and joy. This is what the Bible calls "working out your salvation," expecting to "run" from glory to glory, to go from good to better onto the very best!

If you have read this book and are not yet "born again" or saved, being a child of God, belonging to Jesus, is the very best of the best. And here is your opportunity!

In the book of Romans we read:

If you confess with your mouth the Lord Jesus and believe in your heart that God has raised Him from the dead, you will be saved. For with the heart one believes unto righteousness, and with the mouth confession is made unto salvation.

Romans 10:9-10

Believing that Scripture passage to be true, please pray this prayer with me:

Father God, I am sorry I have sinned and made You sad. I ask You to please, forgive me for all my sins. I believe in my heart that Jesus Christ died for me and has been raised from the dead. I receive You now, Jesus, as my Lord and Savior. Amen.

If you prayed this prayer, congratulations! You have just been saved and have entered into the blood covenant with Christ. You are now a child of God and an heir in the Kingdom of God. Please contact us for a gift.

If you already are a child of God and on your way to heaven, I expect you to make a firm decision today to start operating in the authority and power you are entitled to! Let the Holy Spirit help you mature in all areas of your life and start using the gifts and the anointing you have been given by God in an even greater way. I pray you will be a great blessing and a more powerful tool in the hands of the Lord after having read this book, and that it will help you lead many people to the Lord.

If you have any questions or want to know more about us or about the emotional healing and restoration ministry, please contact us.

I will be very happy to talk with you.

About the Author

D r. Elin Riegel has a background of more than 20 years in business and 19 years in the ministry as an ordained minister.

She also has a Master in Christian Leadership and a Doctor of Ministry and several secular leadership courses.

In 1989 she had a personal encounter with God and was born again.

Then in 1990, God called her to go to Bible School, and she resigned from her position as a buyer for a furniture company with more than $ 30 million turnover and gave up a job that included travelling all over the world.

After finishing 2 years of Bible Studies at Rhema Bible Training Centre in Tulsa Oklahoma, she returned to Norway to help organize a new company.

In 1996 she moved to Spain and started World Impact Ministries that today run Bible Institutes in various places and have students online and onsite from all over the world. Through Destiny College in the USA, World Impact Ministries offers a Master in Christian Leadership.

Almost from the beginning she started to study the blood covenant, and from 1990 she was active in the inner healing ministry in her local church.

Later, the Lord added more and more understanding about inner healing, and today she has been ministering inner healing in several countries of the world.

She is also the president and founder of ICCC Spain (International Christian Chamber of Commerce), a Christian Business Network that exists in more than 65 countries globally.

God has really put the Marketplace ministry on her heart, and she is now responsible for rising up chambers for ICCC in all the Latin American countries.

Dr. Elin Riegel has two daughters who are married and 4 grandchildren. She keeps travelling the world either for inner healing, for the Bible Institute or for ICCC.

Contact Information

Dr. Elin Riegel

World Impact Ministries

Buzón 79 Sierra de Altea

03599 Altea (Alicante)

Spain

Email: info@wiministries.com

Phone: + 34 965 858584

Web: www.wiministries.com

www.ingramcontent.com/pod-product-compliance
Lightning Source LLC
Chambersburg PA
CBHW051839090426
42736CB00011B/1876